# IN THE PINK

BY THE SAME AUTHOR

*FICTION*

FOR ALL THAT I FOUND THERE
THE STEPDAUGHTER
THE FATE OF MARY ROSE
GREAT-GRANNY WEBSTER
CORRIGAN

*NON-FICTION*

DARLING, YOU SHOULDN'T HAVE GONE TO SO MUCH TROUBLE
(WITH ANNA HAYCRAFT)
ON THE PERIMETER

# IN THE PINK

CAROLINE BLACKWOOD

*on hunting*



BLOOMSBURY

First published 1987


Bloomsbury Publishing Ltd, 4 Bloomsbury Place, London WC1A 2QA

British Library Cataloguing in Publication Data

Blackwood, Caroline
In the pink: Caroline Blackwood on hunting
1. Fox-hunting — Great Britain
I. Title
799.2′5974442 SK287.G7

ISBN 0-7475-0050-9

The lines from 'The Early Purges' used
as an epigraph on p. 25 are reprinted
by permission of Faber and Faber Ltd
from *Death of a Naturalist* by
Seamus Heaney.

Printed in Great Britain by
Butler & Tanner Ltd, Frome and London

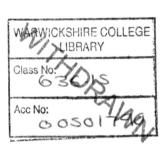

More people are fox-hunting in Britain today than have ever hunted in the history of the sport. Never before has it been so popular — or so unpopular. In the eyes of some purists, the fact that a great many of the hunters participate from their cars may detract aesthetically from the spectacle, and petrol fumes may do nothing to enhance the scent in the 'muzzles' of the hounds, but hunting is an immensely expensive business. Healthy subscriptions of car-hunters are not undervalued.

Distinguished novelist and journalist Caroline Blackwood here presents an intriguing and acerbic investigation into the current state of the ancient pastime and the passions which rage on either side of the fence. We meet Laura, Duchess of Marlborough, who risked serious injury in continuing to ride side-saddle for the effect of her couture. We visit the aggressive vegan of 'Little Heaven' and discover from the head of the League Against Cruel Sports that most of his members were bullied at school. Francis Bacon, Lord Longford and Molly Keane recall their hunting experiences, as do participants, spectators and campaigners of very different leanings.

Unearthed are the ancient rituals, superstitions and satanic legends of the hunt. Oddities of hunting terminology are explained along with the latest on etiquette and snobberies, including the scandalous use Prince Charles made of pink elastic. Topics such as adultery and the hunt, the function of gawdy orange foundation make-up and the 'blooding' of children bring us into the heart of the hunting family. The author's first-hand experiences of car-hunting bring us into the heart of a traffic jam.

This lively, penetrating, and sometimes shocking, study places in full view one of the most controversial issues known to man, woman and beast. Advocates and opponents alike will have to admire its sense of fair play in letting the facts, if not the foxes, speak for themselves.

FOR EVGENIA, IVANA AND SHERIDAN

# Contents

# Introduction

*''Unting is all that's worth living for – all time is lost wot is not spent in 'unting – it is like the hair we breathe – if we have it not we die – it's the sport of kings, the image of war without its guilt.'*

Surtees

'Obviously, the hunting of the fox has been my chief concern,' wrote the late Duke of Beaufort in 1982. In this crisp and confident sentence he summed up his whole life and his attitude towards the universe. It was the Duke's 'obviously' which proved the electric word. It aroused feelings of bemused incomprehension and stronger emotions of murderous anger. The right of the Englishman to fox-hunt, and the right to prevent him from doing so, is a very parochial, very 'English' issue – a quarrel that one might have imagined would have faded in importance in the 1980s. Yet it can still arouse violent passions.

In 1986 two members of an organisation called the Hunt Retribution Squad defiled the Duke of Beaufort's grave, which is to be found in his family's private burial ground near Badminton. While they were trying to dig up his corpse their spade broke. Only this little accident prevented them from carrying out an enterprise which demonstrates the extremism of their anti-hunt position. The two young offenders admitted in court that they were hoping to cut off the late Duke's head in order to send it to Princess Anne.

The Duke was selected as the victim of this grisly attack because his life epitomised everything that many British animal lovers detest. He was impervious to criticism. He claimed that if there was anything better than a bad day's hunting it was a good day's hunting. He encouraged Prince Charles and Princess Anne to ride with his hounds and, even though he is dead and buried (maybe at the moment somewhat precariously), his enemies have not forgiven him. 'Dig deeper for the Duke,' implored the banner slogans of the protesters as they paraded before the Queen at the Badminton Horse Trials recently.

When his grave was vandalised, the Duke's attackers were not only treating him like the thousands of trapped foxes that he'd dug out of the earth in his lifetime; they were also making a symbolic attempt to dig out the evil which they felt lived after him. They were trying to eradicate this evil with a spade, as if they believed that it lay there, literally 'interred within his bones'.

When I first read about the gruesome incident at the Badminton burial ground, I found it not only repulsive but pointless. I felt that the protesters were 'flogging a dead horse'. I had never fox-hunted, nor had I witnessed a fox-hunt, and my only experiences of the chase had been the rare occasions when I had been coerced into following the North Down Harriers when I was a child living in Ulster. They were a bumbling and undistinguished pack and, due to their inefficiency and lack of expertise, the hare never seemed to get caught. For that reason I had never thought of hunting as being very cruel.

However, although the 'pace' of the North Down Harriers was stumbling, I'd still found it too fast and frightening, being a timid and unskilled rider, and I was very happy to give up the chase.

Later, living abroad and in cities, I never gave a thought to hunting or the controversy and moral debate that surround it. I assumed that the sport must now be practised so rarely by so few that the 'saboteurs' were foolish to use it as a pivot for an animal lovers' protest.

I then learned that more people are fox-hunting in Britain today than have ever hunted before in the history of the sport.

I found it astonishing that this archaic activity has managed to flourish in an era in which one would have expected modern obstacles, such as motorways, ring roads and by-passes, fence-wiring and urban development, galloping inflation and organised anti-blood sport groups, to have guaranteed its extinction. I was told that the whole issue of fox-hunting in Mrs Thatcher's Britain contains a paradox: the sport has never been so popular as it is today; perversely, never in its history has it been so violently unpopular.

This unlikely situation roused my curiosity; I wanted to understand the conflict between the hunt and the anti's. I started to talk to passionate advocates of fox-hunting and passionate opponents, and as I did so I felt that I was learning about a clash that has many similarities to a religious war.

# 1

# The Last Great Master

*'Like a dog, he hunts in dreams.'*

Tennyson

If fox-hunting can be described as a religion, the late Duke of Beaufort was certainly one of its last great Popes. He devoted a lifetime to spreading its gospels and demonstrating its beauties by his flawless example. His long and happy career was entirely devoted to the killing of the fox: when he suffered a heart attack at the age of eighty-three he was following his hounds in a car.

You only need a thumb-nail sketch of his life to begin to understand why many animal lovers wish to desecrate his memory. Not only was he one of the most passionate and courageous huntsmen that Great Britain has ever produced, but he was descended from a long and distinguished line of equally dedicated hunters. He had Plantagenet blood and was the direct descendant of that fierce implacable hunter, John of Gaunt, the son of Edward III. If there had not been some ancient stain of illegitimacy blotting his escutcheon, the late Duke of Beaufort would have been the rightful King of England. He was never to ascend to the English throne, but he established himself as unchallenged King of the hunt, and many of his followers and admirers felt that this title was as worthy of respect as that of any crowned head in Europe.

The Duke was christened Henry, but all his life he was known only by his nickname, 'Master'. Even the authoritarian title that he chose for himself makes opponents of blood sports long to reach for the spade. At the age of nine he was given a pack of hounds by his father and early childhood photographs show him as a grinning little imp in a velvet jockey cap triumphantly waving in the air the head of a bleeding animal.

When the Duke started his career as a child hunter people would come up to the little boy and ask, 'Where are you drawing today, Master?'

The use of the word 'drawing' has provided many in jokes for huntsmen to laugh at. There are tales of farmers who have been asked for permission to 'draw' their woods. Unfamiliar with the term, the innocents have assumed the riders were hoping to do a charcoal sketch or a watercolour using their beautiful trees as a model. In reality the horsemen were asking to be allowed to ride through the woodlands with their hounds, hoping to scare up some unfortunate fox.

When the young Henry was first addressed as 'Master' he loved the name so much that he decided to adopt it for ever. In later life his wife and his friends only ever called him 'Master', as did the Queen and the Queen Mother. He always preferred the informal title to the formal one of 'Your Grace'.

All his life he had the initials MFH1 emblazoned on the registration plates of his car. MFH stood for Master of Foxhounds and the number one established his prime position in the world of the hunt. 'I am honoured to be called Master,' he said.

Appropriately enough, his father, the 9th Duke of Beaufort, was pulling on his hunting boots when he received the news of Master's birth. Undeterred, he continued with his elaborate sartorial preparations for the hunt. He kept the thrilling news that he now had a male heir to take over the mastership of the famous Beaufort hounds to himself. It apparently never occurred to him to go to the bedside of his wife and his newborn son, nor did he take the time to make enquiries as to their health.

He rode off to the meet as usual. In a slack moment in the hunt when the hounds temporarily had lost the scent, he told his followers that he had just given birth to a son. 'May we give three cheers, Your Grace?' Will Dale, his huntsman, asked him. 'Certainly not,' the Duke replied, 'you might frighten the hounds.'

When Master grew up, he inherited the same philosophical attitude to life as his father. The horse, the hounds and the hunt must always come first.

The 10th Duke of Beaufort was to act as master to his own hounds for four decades, the longest mastership in British hunting history. When he was eighty he was still in the saddle, holding the horn and wearing the green coat of the Beaufort Hunt. The buttons on his coat were two hundred years old and were transferred from coat to coat as he outwore them.

For most of his adult life, this bluff and dedicated man hunted six days a week. During one period he hunted fox-cubs twice a day. He was up hunting them in the early mornings and he hunted them again in the late evening. He was able to joke that sometimes he had hunted nine days a week. 'Nothing is as fun as that was,' he declared.

In 1939, when he was called up for the Army reserve, he went out for one final cub-hunt, fearing that it might be his last hunt on earth. In an interview with the sporting magazine the *Field*, he described the experience. 'We had a very good day running across the aerodrome area. A man came out with a gun (they had just started work on those aerodromes). A fox came out too and the man said, "Shall I shoot him?" I said, "If you shoot him, I'll shoot you!"'

The soldier with the gun saw that Master was serious. The Duke was a genial man, but he had an evil temper if anything spoiled his hunting. The soldier retreated into his aerodrome, and Master went on with the chase. In his interview he doesn't say how many cubs he killed. Presumably it was quite a few. He was able to recollect with nostalgia: 'I always remember that the good God had given me a wonderful day on the last one before the War.'

After his military call-up, Henry Beaufort was fortunate. One of the fittest men in the country, he was declared unfit to serve by the Army because he developed a duodenal ulcer. His critics believe that he developed this nervous condition unconsciously, out of fear that war would deprive him of his hunting.

When he was a teenager the First World War had thwarted his great ambition of becoming Master of the Eton Beagles. The European conflict had produced such serious shortages in Great Britain that it became impossible to feed the Eton hounds.

In the Second World War, however, Master's hunting was not so badly affected, and throughout the Battle of Britain he was able to continue to wage his private war against the fox. He struggled valiantly to keep his hounds hunting, although the new shortages and the conscription of his hunting staff made it such a struggle that he had to restrict his hunting times. In wartime he held his meets only four days a week. He evacuated fifty hounds, despatching them to safety in Canada, presumably at great cost. He felt that even if Great Britain was destroyed by the Germans, and his kennels at Badminton were bombed, one of her noblest assets, the Beaufort hounds, would carry on her great tradition on the other side of the Atlantic.

The war presented Master with another, most unusual problem. His wife, Mary Beaufort, was the niece of Queen Mary, who descended on him with an entourage of fifty servants, having chosen his stately home, Badminton, as a suitable place to sit out the war and avoid the dangers of the London air-raids. After the royal invasion had taken place, the Duke and Duchess were left with only two bedrooms at their disposal.

The royal biographer, James Pope Hennessy, described Queen Mary as being 'fundamentally very, very German; the two things she liked most were destruction and order'. The destructive side of her nature was to affect the lives of the Duke and Duchess of Beaufort, for they soon discovered that they were unable to go out for a day's hunting without receiving an unpleasant shock on their return. Queen Mary had a passion for felling trees, and when they came home tired and muddied it was to find to their distress that yet another beautiful tree on the Badminton estate had been axed at the Queen's command.

James Pope Hennessy describes one episode, which conjures up the problems that confronted Master during the wartime sojourn of his royal relative.

On leaving for hunting one day, the Duchess said, 'Now Aunt Mary, remember that the shrubs outside the stable wall are not to be touched.' The next day Queen Mary led her round to the stables and every shrub was gone, revealing a naked wall which then had to be cemented and painted. Before the Duchess could say anything, Queen Mary, like a naughty child, said quickly, 'I'm glad you like my yesterday's work.'

The Germanic, order-loving side of the Queen also caused inconvenience for the Duke and Duchess. While they were out hunting, the Queen liked to collect all the agricultural implements that she found in the fields on the Badminton estate. She would arrange to have the farm equipment brought back to the stable-yard, not realising that it had been left out in the fields for sound agricultural reasons.

When impeccably run hunting stables were reduced to something closely resembling a junk yard by the daily whims of the Queen, a terrible burden was thrown on the gallant and ancient grooms who were battling to preserve pre-war hunting standards during a difficult period when all the younger men had been recruited into the armed forces. But Beaufort survived the vicissitudes of Queen Mary's wartime evacuation, and another Master of Fox-hounds, Sir Peter Farquhar, praised Master's activities when the Second World War ended. 'After the war he dedicated his life to try to help the younger generation to get everything going again.'

Master stated his post-war feelings very plainly. 'We have fought – and won – two world wars for our right to be free. Now all we want is to be able to enjoy our field sports without any interference from people who often, more's the pity, do not in the least understand what it is they are opposing.'

Just before his death, he grew frail and was no longer able to ride. He staunchly continued to kill foxes from a Land Rover, shooting them through the window with a gun.

Here the Pope of fox-hunting proved fallible. Purists of the sport consider it a criminal act to kill a fox without first chasing it on horseback. Anyone who destroys a fox by other means is described as a 'vulpicide'. This word arouses emotions of horror and disgust similar to those evoked by the image of the matricide.

In his novel *The American Senator*, Anthony Trollope creates a scene that neatly depicts the horror of the huntsman when he stumbles on an act of vulpicide:

> The Senator and Morton followed close on the steps of Lord Rufford and Captain Glomax [the Master] and were thus able to make their way into the centre of the crowd. There, on a clean sward of grass, laid out as carefully as though he were a royal child prepared for burial was – a dead fox. 'It's pi'son, my lord; it's pi'son to a moral,' said Bean, who, as keeper of the wood, was bound to vindicate himself, and his master and the wood. 'Feel of him, how stiff he is.' A good many did feel, but Lord Rufford stood still and looked at the poor victim in silence. 'It's easy knowing how he came by it,' said Bean.
>
> The men around gazed into each other's faces with a sad tragic air, as though the occasion were one which at the first blush was too melancholy for words . . . the dreadful word 'vulpicide' was heard from various lips with an oath or two before it. 'It makes me sick of my

own land to think it should be done so near,' said Larry Twentyman, who had just come up. Mr Runciman declared that they must set their wits to work not only to find the criminal but to prove the crime against him, and offered to subscribe a couple of sovereigns on the spot to a common fund to be raised for the purpose. 'I don't know what is to be done with a country like this,' said Captain Glomax, who, as an itinerant, was not averse to cast a slur upon the land of his present sojourn.

'I don't remember anything like it on my property before,' said the Lord, standing up for his own estate and the country at large.

'Nor in the hunt,' said young Hampton. 'Of course, such a thing may happen anywhere. They had foxes poisoned in the Pytchley last year.'

'It shows d—— bad feeling somewhere,' said the Master.

In the nineteenth century, if a gamekeeper or farmer displayed vulpicidal tendencies, he soon regretted it. A tenant farmer would be evicted; a gamekeeper would be imprisoned or suffer some other severe punishment. To this day, many tenant farmers living in Leicestershire have a curious clause in their leases, which contracts them to do everything possible to assist the hunt, and therefore legally restrains them from shooting foxes.

Laura, Duchess of Marlborough, used to be a passionate fox-hunter in the 1920s and 1930s. She remembers being sent 'off the field' because her current husband, the Earl of Dudley, was vulpicidal. 'Eric always shot foxes on the estate. He did it because of the pheasants. But it wasn't *my* fault . . . '

Being dismissed from the hunt and told to go home by the master is the worst humiliation that a fox-hunter can suffer. He or she feels the shame of an officer who has been reduced to the ranks. Although the humiliation of the Duchess of Marlborough took place over forty years ago, the injustice that she had suffered still rankles and she remembers the episode with anger. So Henry Beaufort's lapse in old age was a serious one as viewed by his fellow huntsmen.

Nevertheless, his followers forgave him. No doubt, they remembered his previous flawless record. On occasions when his hounds were tearing some fox apart they would transport the old Duke to the spot so that he could sit in a wheelchair and enjoy the kill.

When Master died in 1984 the nation mourned him as if he were a second Churchill. The newspapers and the sporting magazines ran over-sized black banner headlines: FAREWELL TO MASTER . . . THANK YOU, MASTER . . . ONE OF THE ROYAL FAMILY'S FAVOURITE PEOPLE DIES . . . THE NOBLEST MASTER OF THEM ALL.

Henry Beaufort's obituaries were extraordinary. He was praised for believing, like Jorrocks, that 'All time is lost, wot is not spent in 'unting.' He was praised for his horsemanship, his courage and his courtesy. He was praised for his good memory. (Even at eighty-two he could still remember the faces of those who had attended his hunt.) Master was commended for his breeding; both the way he bred his hounds and his own breeding. One article in *Horse and Hound* began, 'Even today it is almost impossible not to be important if you are a Duke. The 10th Duke of Beaufort was a very important person.'

Master was praised for his 'zest for life', for his loyalty 'to his family and his tenants'. The Master of Fox-hounds, Sir Peter Farquhar, wrote, 'The Duke's death has been the day I have dreaded most.' Another MFH, Captain R. E. Wallace, observed, 'It was ever an inspiration to see Master hunt his hounds. The connection between him and those bitches, the skill of the whippers-in and the acceleration with which the whole outfit went away was an example which could never be excelled.'

Some of the writers of Master's obituaries became over

effusive. In *Horse and Hound* a tribute signed 'Loriner' went like this:

> Yes, he was as human as the rest of us, despite the fact that he was descended from none other than the great John of Gaunt. Perhaps the words, very slightly adapted, that Shakespeare gave to John of Gaunt's nephew, Richard II, might be the most appropriate:
>
> *You have mistook me all this while;*
> *I have lived with bread like you, feel want,*
> *Taste grief, need friends: subjected thus*
> *How can you say to me, I am a* DUKE.
>
> But he was a Duke – just the sort of Duke we wanted; and in the horse world we shall miss him greatly. Thank you, 'Master'!

In the *Spectator*, Simon Blow maundered on about the late Duke with much the same choked and elegiac emotion. 'Many will recall the lovely moment caught on television when he spread out his coat for the Queen, to sit on the grass, which was very wet.'

The same writer was less effective when his prose throbbed with nostalgia, as he valiantly tried to give a poignant example of the late Duke's wit. 'But what of the man within? On the complicated subject of Life, he remained a lovable innocent. His humour was always straightforward and sparked off by what we might call "good, clean fun". To a lady who had amused him at dinner he guffawed in jest, "If you say that again, I'll prod you with this fork!"'

In the same obituary the 10th Duke of Beaufort was extolled for 'sticking to the enduring values of our ancient squirearchy'. Simon Blow concluded his 'homage' to the dead huntsman with these stirring words, 'I hope that Master has now found his pastures Elysian.'

Henry Beaufort's memorial service at the Guards' Chapel was attended by Prince Philip, representing the Queen, Prince Charles and Princess Diana, the Queen Mother and Princess Anne and all the royal Dukes. Elgar's Nimrod theme was played, as was Haydn's Hunt Symphony. Lines from Master's favourite poet, Will Ogilvie, had been printed on the funeral programmes which were distributed round the pews.

*Far on the hill is the horn still blowing . . .*
*Far on the steep are the hounds still strung . . .*

Simon Blow attended the service and described the prayers that were said on the occasion. 'We gave thanks for his mastership of man, and horse and hounds.' Spoken in 1984 they were unusual prayers.

When he was alive, Master always insisted that, apart from a war, there was nothing that united a country as much as hunting. The League Against Cruel Sports and the British Field Sports Society are now making contradictory statements about the percentage of British citizens who would like the sport to be declared illegal. The claims and counter-claims of these two warring factions are predictable. Both parties maintain that the great mass of the nation is on their side. The fact that their statistics are contradictory proves that Master was wrong. The hunt is obviously not now uniting the people of Great Britain. On the contrary, it would appear to be dividing them.

When Master took up the pen rather than the reins his style had none of the masterly pace of his own bold lifestyle. His prose was halting and inelegant, but when he was writing on his favourite subject he knew how to whip up his rhetoric.

In the *Field* he argued with eloquence: 'Field sports are part of our heritage, every bit as much as are all the fine buildings that many of us fight to preserve . . . If the critics of fox-hunting think they can, by a stroke of the pen, make us give up the sport our fathers have enjoyed for hundreds of years, they are completely ignorant of the British character.'

When Master made this kind of statement he was thumbing his autocratic nose at the animal rights groups who loathe the cruelty of the fox-hunt. He mocked the League Against Cruel Sports, the hunt saboteurs, and the most extreme of these organisations, the Hunt Retribution Squad. They saw the Duke of Beaufort as an unrepentant Mengele, intent on tormenting foxes, just as the Nazi doctor had been obsessed with torturing twins. It was for this reason that two of the most fanatical of his opponents tracked him down to his grave.

I asked fox-hunting friends and admirers of Master what they felt about the incident at Badminton. They naturally found it frightening, but felt that Master would have *liked* to have had his head dug up and sent to Princess Anne. At first this startled me, and I found it very difficult to understand this interpretation of the late Duke's point of view.

I could only assume that this claim was meant to be taken metaphorically. Master surely would not have liked the idea of poor Princess Anne having her peaceful breakfast of toast and marmalade ruined as she opened her gift parcel and a putrefied, grinning ducal head rolled out on to her snowy tablecloth. But he would have liked the idea of his head being resurrected. As it came out of the grave, he would have felt that all the 'values of the ancient British squirearchy' were being resurrected with it.

Lord Byron had only scorn for the intrepid ancestral squires who originally promoted those values:

*For what were all these country patriots born?*
*To hunt, and vote and raise the price of corn?*

But Henry Beaufort adulated them, and apparently would have been happy to have his coffin excavated if his exhumation would help to promote the values that he so treasured.

He also might have applauded the creepy act of the saboteurs, seeing it as a form of sport. Even if he saw it as a plebeian sport, it was certainly a blood sport, so he would have had to approve of it from that point of view.

And thinking about the late Duke's astonishing ability to turn the most hostile of attacks on his way of life to his own delight, I felt that even in death that incorrigible huntsman would always defeat the League Against Cruel Sports. He would always elude the most dedicated of the hunt saboteurs. They could dig him up as much as they liked, but Master, still blithely hunting somewhere in the Elysian Fields, by applauding the hunting element in their protest, would manage to master it.

# 2

# The League Against Cruel Sports

*'Prevention of cruelty talk cuts ice in town where they consider death unnatural, but on well-run farms pests have to be kept down.'*

Seamus Heaney

In the dilapidated office of the headquarters of the League Against Cruel Sports, which is situated in Southwark, London, the memoirs of the late Duke of Beaufort are to be found in a special glass case.

The League is right to cherish this book, which is getting increasingly hard to obtain and now has a great scarcity value. For those who love its contents and its approach, it is a classic – a volume beyond price.

When Beaufort's memoirs were initially published in 1981, they reached a very small but élitist audience. By the nature of the material that the Duke covered, his book was doomed to be a work of very limited appeal. His fox-hunting admirers gave it to each other for Christmas, but it did not go into a second printing, and paperback companies made no determined efforts to obtain it.

The members of the League Against Cruel Sports were very strict in their protection of the late Duke's memoirs and I was not allowed to borrow them. Their rules forbade me to remove the book from the premises, so I could only read it under supervision in the reading room.

All the other literature to be found at the League's headquarters can be bought and the proceeds then go to the cause.

All its books deal with different aspects of cruelty to animals and many of them contain gruesome material. But the League did not seem to treasure any of them as it treasured the late Duke's memoirs. If a Jewish organisation was to have a copy of *Mein Kampf* in its headquarters, it might be equally fussy in its refusal to allow the book to be taken from its reading room. It is intelligent to treasure the enemy's Bible. It is always there to be referred to and it is useful to the fighters, for it serves to remind them of exactly what it is they are fighting against.

'They pretend they don't breed hounds for slowness,' a League worker said to me, 'it is a bloody lie! You will find it there in Beaufort's book. He admits it himself. He is proud of it. They breed hounds for slowness so that they can prolong the agony for the fox. Sadists in pink coats . . . that's what I call them.'

I never reached the part of the late Duke's memoirs where he admits to breeding hounds for slowness. I was eventually defeated by the sheer size of an opus which records the life of a man who had devoted every waking second to the killing of the fox and the breeding and cross-breeding of hounds.

The Duke's hobbies were highly intricate and he expounded their joys at enormous length. The book contained numerous detailed accounts of 'good days' that he'd had with his hounds. He even described some of the 'good days' that his father, the 9th Duke of Beaufort, had enjoyed before him and a 'good day' read about, rather than experienced, can make for unstimulating reading.

'From Lyde Green Head, Bristol, two rings in the Vale (15 miles) then to the hills, first to Sir William Codrington's woods at Doddington, then to the Duke's woods at Didmarton, Hawkesbury Upton, Kilcot, and killed between Kilcot and Frocester. Found at 7.30 and killed at 4.00. All the Field were thrown out and 6 people out of 17 (hounds) in at the death.'

Beaufort did make some mention of breeding hounds for 'nose and stern'. I wondered if one were to breed a hound for 'stern' whether one would be breeding it for slowness? His memoirs were giving me a headache and I found I couldn't care.

I would have abandoned the Duke's memoirs much sooner if I had not been reading them under the supervision of the League. I feared its workers would see me as unconscientious if I failed to persevere with his reminiscences. They might think I was lazily evading the real nitty-gritty of the whole subject of fox-hunting. But following the late Duke down his long memory lane of 'good hunting days' was an exhausting and tedious occupation.

There was something surrealistic about struggling with this unreadable book in the headquarters of the League, where every wall has a poster depicting the gory end of some unfortunate mink, badger or fox. The reading room is rather grim, with the austere and embattled atmosphere sometimes created by groups who have chosen to sacrifice all creature comforts to a worthy cause.

Visitors can see bloody videos at the League. A few years ago the organisation found a superb rider who was happy to act as an undercover agent and ride with the hunt in order to spy on its activities. The League's hunting mole rode with several fashionable packs throughout the season and became a popular and admired member of the field. In the evenings he attended the hunt dinners and drank their port. He also consumed the succulent meat that the hunt's table provided for him. He then slipped off secretly to the lavatory and put his fingers down his throat. He vomited up the acid froth of beef and kidneys and veal that he had just eaten – the League's spy was a very strict vegetarian.

He asked permission to film the 'kill' of various foxes and stags. The hunts allowed him to do this because they assumed he wanted to have the films as a personal memento of past happy occasions. They assumed that he would treasure these videos and re-run them at his leisure, bringing pleasure to his children and grandchildren.

The identity of the equestrian spy was not revealed to me, and I assumed that his undercover work for the League was continuing. Having got out his camera, he double-crossed the hunting fraternity. He handed over his videos to the League, which now uses them as anti-hunt propaganda and shows them at its London headquarters.

The most telling photograph that the undercover agent brought back to the League was a picture of a dead hound lying in a feeding trough. The hunt has always denied that it feeds its hounds on old and worn-out hounds who have 'had their day'. The mole's photograph, for which the League is very grateful, suggests that these denials are untrue. The practice of recycling old hounds may be economical with the ever rising costs of meat, but it creates a distasteful image. It did occur to me, however, that the undercover agent with his duplicitous nature might have planted the dead hound in the feeding trough in order to take a snap of it. If he was prepared to go through the agonies of regurgitating the hunt's roast beef, there seemed to be no limit as to what he might do to discredit them.

I still felt apprehensive as I waited to be shown the videos. They were unlikely to be faked and a young man who was working for the League informed me that many Members of Parliament had fainted when they were shown this gruesome evidence. I was selfishly glad to discover that the videos were not as effective as they were meant to be.

The mole was not a good film maker and his pictures were fuzzy and indistinct. Presumably he'd done much of his filming on horseback. He had concentrated only on photographing the 'kills' and had made no attempt to capture the thundering beauty of the chase which must have preceded the deaths of the unlucky stags and foxes. Perhaps he'd been too frightened to show the spectacular and exciting side of the hunt for fear that he might show the sport sympathetically to his viewers and his videos would then become propagandist in a manner directly opposed to his intention.

By censoring all the pageantry of the hunt, the animal deaths captured by the mole on video looked distasteful and sordid, but they were neither shocking nor moving. Possibly film is an unsatisfactory medium for portraying the agony and terror of the hunted creature – the concrete celluloid image has less emotional impact than images in the imagination. On the videos a fox was running and then there was a skirmish with the hounds (again a fuzzy picture due to faulty photography). Then the huntsman was triumphantly holding up a fox's bleeding head, and though the shot was nasty the effect was anti-climactic.

Only the cries of the foxes on the soundtrack shocked the audience in the way that the mole had intended. The high-pitched, child-like screams that these animals let out as the hounds literally tore them apart echoed in one's head. I wondered if it was these terrible cries of pain that had made the Members of Parliament faint.

The screams of the murdered foxes seemed to go on echoing round the League's reading room as I sat ploughing miserably through the Duke of Beaufort's memoirs long after the videos had ended.

I tried to imagine the agonies the mole must have gone through when his double-dealing spy role forced him to attend the hunt balls. Had he found himself dancing waltz after waltz with satin-clad, horse-faced hunting ladies?

I remembered attending a hunt ball in Dublin, given by the Meath. A waiter came in carrying a huge decorated salmon on a plate. The huntsmen encouraged him by shouting hunting cries. 'Hold hard!' 'Go forrard!' They thought themselves very funny. How could the spy have enjoyed all that? Surely he must have loathed the raucousness of all the red-coated men as they danced the conga, drank champagne, blew hunting horns and boasted about the 'kills' they had been in on. The scarlet of their coats could never have looked 'pink' to the mole. It must have seemed blood-stained.

As I contemplated the miseries that the hunting spy had

very probably endured in order to produce the videos, I wondered if his whole altruistic enterprise had been worth it. Technically, his films were unmemorable examples of photography, but the sad little screams of the hunted foxes were still echoing in my head. I would never forget them. I felt that on balance the spy had done a more persuasive propaganda job for his anti-hunt position than the Duke of Beaufort's ponderous memoirs achieved for the sport that he had lived for.

I wondered if the late Duke would have liked to have known that his life's great literary work would end up in a glass case in a grim London suburb far from the Elysian Fields he had always frequented. At least the League was 'conserving' his memoirs and he'd always been passionately keen on 'conservation'. The League Against Cruel Sports was certainly preserving a bit of our 'national heritage' by guarding his memoirs so strictly. It was unlikely that even the most fervent huntsman or hound breeder had given his book the attention that it was afforded in the reading room. Visitors to the League's headquarters treated the Duke of Beaufort's memoirs as if they were sacred. They gave them all the rapt and devoted attention that Irish monks accord the Book of Kells.

# 3

# The Opposition

*'Fight the good fight with all thy might.'*
Hymns Ancient and Modern

The League Against Cruel Sports is a splinter group which has broken away from the Royal Society for the Prevention of Cruelty to Animals. Like the Fabians, who formed a protest group – the Humanitarians' League – around the turn of the century, the current League challenges the Royal Society because it does nothing to prevent cruelty to wild animals and protects only domesticated beasts such as the cat, dog and horse.

The Humanitarians' League was soon discredited because its members were considered to be crazy and dangerous. Not only did they oppose fox-hunting, but they were in favour of prison reform, rights for women, vegetarianism and socialism. They were also pacifists and opposed to capital punishment – they protested against Great Britain's entry into the First World War.

Conventional society at that time considered their stance against fox-hunting to be the most heinous of all their delinquent positions. The Humanitarians' League, in turn, objected to the fact that the very same red-faced magistrates who sat on the bench meting out punishments to those who were on trial for flogging their donkey had just come back from a good day's hunting.

The League's membership soon diminished and it collapsed

through lack of financial support. Bernard Shaw wrote a squib in its defence, suggesting that Great Britain should take up seasonal child-hunting. He took the view that if British society were not so hypocritical many people would admit that they saw their children as pests, just as they did foxes. He felt that child-hunting would provide sport for the populace. The average child would be better fed if it was bred to be hunted, and the child survivors who escaped society's 'culling' would help to build a strong and victorious nation.

The League Against Cruel Sports has taken up the Humanitarians' fight. It continues to criticise the Royal Society for the Prevention of Cruelty to Animals, which allows the Queen to be its patron while her children hunt. The League keeps a vigilant watch on the sporting activities of Prince Charles and Princess Anne. Its findings show that Prince Charles has hunted with forty-two different packs, and in 1983 it reported that he was hunting as often as twice a week. The League distributes this kind of information to the media, hoping to stir up a mood of public revulsion that will bring support to its cause. In 1972 it commissioned an opinion poll to establish what percentage of the British population wanted Princess Anne to hunt. The results were satisfactory from the League's point of view. Some 48 per cent thought she ought not to hunt, while 37 per cent thought she should be allowed to do what she wanted to. *The Times* stated: 'The Princess should be granted the widest freedom to follow her own bent and shape her own life.'

John Bryant, who is one of the senior officers of the League, has little sympathy with the idea that the individual should be allowed to hunt the fox as part of his or her personal freedom. 'What happens if the individual likes molesting little children?' he asked me. 'What happens if some idiot gets a kick from setting a kitten on fire? Can we just sit back and say they have a right to follow their own bent? Can we say they should be given the widest freedom to shape their own lives? The fox should be given legal protection against the cruelty of these people. It should be treated like the molested child and the tortured kitten.'

John Bryant is the son of a farmer and was born in Devon. The fox-hunting community likes to claim that all opponents of its sport come from cities, and are therefore ignorant of the hallowed ways of the countryside and have no respect for its laws.

Bryant insists that those who work for his organisation come from both the city and the country. They have only one factor in common – they were all bullied at school. 'You'll find that almost everyone who works for the League was put through hell at school,' he told me. 'They have a horror of the cruel gang coming down on the defenceless individual. That is why they all identify with the poor fox.'

The League receives generous financial support from homosexuals. 'A lot of gays feel that society is ganging up against them. They feel that society wants to hunt them to death.' It is also supported financially by the proverbial 'rich old ladies'. The same wealthy, almost mythical characters who once left their money to the cats' home now feel that the fox is more deserving. They make large donations, and they leave the League legacies in their wills.

The League has been beset by the same problems that have afflicted many other worthy protest organisations. It has been forced to dissociate itself from the most ardent and extreme of its supporters. 'Some of the hunt saboteurs want to kill a huntsman. How can we go along with that?' John Bryant asked me. 'The League is asking people to show more compassion. Where is the compassion in killing a huntsman?'

He also disapproves of other methods that the extremists advocate in their committed battle against the hunt. 'If people put trip wires in front of the horses and poison the hounds – we see that as cruelty to animals. A hound has as much right to live as a fox.'

John Bryant has none of the fanatical hysteria that is manifested by some of the anti's. 'I think fox-hunting is evil,' he said, 'but I don't think that everyone who hunts is evil.' Bernard Shaw took exactly the same position when he wrote, 'I know many sportsmen and none of them are ferocious. I have known many humanitarians and they are all ferocious.'

John Bryant told me an anecdote which illustrated the ambiguities of his relationship with the hunt. He was once in Devonshire when he came across a goat lying in a lane. The goat had been horribly injured, presumably it had been struck by a car. 'I immediately took the poor animal up to the hunt kennels,' he said. 'I knew they'd give it the proper care – they'd get it the best vets – see that its legs were put in the right splints and all that. And the hunt were wonderful to that goat, and yet the same people will tear a stag or a fox apart!'

He seemed to dislike the 'terrier men' who work for the hunt almost more than he disliked most huntsmen. The terrier men follow the hounds in a car with dogs and spades and, when a fox goes to ground, they put their fierce little terriers down the earth where it has taken refuge. A vicious animal fight takes place underground. Sometimes the terriers tear chunks of flesh from the fox and sometimes the frightened fox bites off the nose of one of the dogs or blinds it. If the terriers are defeated the terrier men 'earth-stop' or block up the escape route of the fox. Then they get out their spades and dig it out of its tunnel, whereupon it is destroyed by the waiting hounds.

'The terrier men are disgusting,' John Bryant said to me. 'Most of them aren't even paid to do the work they do. They do it for free – they enjoy it so much. You ought to see them sitting in their Land Rovers just waiting for their moment of glory when a fox goes to ground.' He described one of the cruel practices that many terrier men go in for. They capture a fox and lock it up in a stable. Every day they let their dogs loose for a few minutes with the imprisoned animal. The terriers rehearse on the live fox, using it as their dummy. They get a tantalising taste of its blood as they take great lumps out of its flesh. This daily rehearsal is meant to give them a blood lust so they will put up a good fight on the hunting field.

Bryant showed me a distressing photograph of a fox that had been the victim of the terrier men. His organisation had bought it from a terrier man to stop it being tormented any further – they had bribed him to release it.

'I've hardly ever seen an animal in a worse state when we first got it,' Bryant said. 'It was horrible to see what they'd done to it. Its whole body was one big mass of wounds and scars. All its legs had been broken and they'd set them all wrong so that the poor creature couldn't walk. The terriers had taken out one of its eyes. The pain that animal must have endured – it doesn't bear thinking about.' Apparently the terrier man had been quite happy to sell his victim fox. 'He knew he could always get another one,' Bryant said with bitterness.

The League had placed the tortured fox with a family who now adored it. It was living on their sofa and they were making a great fuss of it. The story of this unhappy fox at least had a comparatively fairy-tale ending.

'But other foxes are being tortured,' Bryant said. 'And the 'kennel men' often do exactly the same thing as the terrier men. They let their young hounds loose with a captured fox. They like to let their young hounds get a taste for blood.'

While I was talking to him at the headquarters of the League Against Cruel Sports, a woman telephoned and asked Bryant if it was illegal to destroy moles by laying traps for them. She wanted to report one of her neighbours. 'I'm afraid it's not illegal,' he answered. 'There's nothing you can do about it – moles are not legally protected.'

When he was younger John Bryant and his followers used to be active non-violent hunt saboteurs. 'We used to run in front of the hounds in order to break the scent so that the fox could escape. We used to leave trails of aniseed to confuse the hounds.'

He found that it was often the loutish foot followers who

behaved with the most violence towards the saboteurs. 'We were more often beaten up by the foot followers than we were attacked by the riders.'

Although some huntsmen agreed with the joint Master of the Essex Union Hunt when he declared, 'Horsewhipping a hunt saboteur is rather like beating a wife. They are both private matters,' Bryant found that others rather admired these strange young men who were prepared to risk their own lives to save the life of a fox. The huntsmen knew the dangers the saboteurs risked by running in front of the stampede of the hounds once they'd been whipped into a frenzy for the kill. They also knew the dangers of arousing the angry passions of the riders, by creating a *coitus interruptus* for those caught up in the boiling excitement of the chase.

I wondered if the admiration that some of the huntsmen apparently felt for the saboteurs was similar to the affectionate admiration that the huntsman has often seemed to feel for the fox.

In hunting prints and literature the fox frequently comes out on top. 'Good old wily Reynard' with his supernatural cunning is presented as the worthy adversary. He is depicted sitting at the top of a tree drinking champagne while the huntsmen lie in a ditch. He frequently appears dressed as the huntsman with top hat, stock, horn and whip, and he is placed in some position of superiority. He makes his escape in unlikely places. He jumps into the open back of a laundry van and fools the hounds as they pass him on the road. He hides up a woman's skirt. He is presented lovingly in all manner of situations and the hunt pays homage to his wiles.

It seemed as though once the saboteurs were running for their lives in front of the hounds they could be viewed as foxes and in their ambiguous role of 'the beloved quarry' some of the huntsmen could raise their caps to them.

The hunting community sees the saboteurs as even more cunning than foxes. Many of the 'sabs' have learnt to blow the hunting horn just as well as any huntsman. Although the uninstructed think that you only have to pick it up and give it a puff, the instrument is a very difficult one to master. The saboteurs take months conscientiously practising. They do their breathing exercises and eventually learn to reproduce all the different notes with which a huntsman instructs his hounds. They attend the various meets carrying tape machines. Having taped all the hunting cries and varying horn signals they perfect their technique, to the dismay of their neighbours, by reproducing them at home. Later they follow the hounds shrieking perfect 'Huic halloas' and blowing horn instructions which misdirect the hounds and send them far away from the path of the fox.

John Bryant has not been an active saboteur for many years. He no longer puts himself in a position in which, 'like a wife', he can be horsewhipped according to the 'private' persuasion of the individual horseman.

He fights the hunt from the city, using political weapons now rather than aniseed.

The League Against Cruel Sports publishes an anti-blood sport newspaper, and brings pressure to bear on politicians. It buys up land in strategic positions so that it can interfere with the progress of all the various hunts. One hunt was recently fined £50,000 when its hounds ran over land owned by the League. This was an important test case. Hunt balls with highly priced tickets were held all over Great Britain so that the hunt could raise money to pay this massive fine.

The League also encourages individuals to sue the hunt if it lets its hounds run over their fields and it gives them legal advice on how to proceed. The hunt takes the League's activities very seriously. If farmers who have no strong feelings about fox-hunting start bringing law-suits against the hunt just because they are attracted by the money they can gain from a case, the whole future of British fox-hunting will be jeopardised.

John Bryant gave up active protest on the field when his group was joined by swarms of punks. 'A lot of idiots started to turn up calling themselves hunt protesters and they had green and red spiked hair and safety pins through their noses and all that . . . I knew they didn't care about cruelty to animals. They were just hoping for a fight . . . I didn't want to be associated with them. They created a very bad image. And if you want to achieve anything worthwhile it's a mistake to let yourself get a disgusting image – look what's happened to the Greenham women. They have a perfectly sane and moral position, but they have not cared enough about their image. If you want to beat the tweeds and green wellington brigade you have to have more tweeds and green wellingtons than they do.'

# 4

# 'Little Heaven'

*'Men are never so good or bad as their opinions.'*
Sir James Mackintosh

'I don't see anything wrong with killing a huntsman,' a hunt saboteur said to me.

Tim Morgan is a 'vegan' who runs a sanctuary for animals in the north of England. He owns a herd of cows and refuses to drink milk. He keeps turkeys and hens, but believes that it is cruel to eat eggs. 'Vegans' eat no dairy products.

His sanctuary is on a run-down farm and is surrounded by caravans. Girls with long dresses and flowing 1960s hair waft around him paying him homage and acting as handmaidens. They treat him as a guru. When I visited 'Little Heaven', as it is called, a girl brought me a cup of instant coffee laced with soya milk. As a beverage it was curiously sour and disgusting.

Tim Morgan had the unhealthy complexion with which those who restrict their diet to the very purest of ingredients are often oddly cursed. He was wearing a T-shirt that carried the slogan, 'Don't split hares.' In Leicestershire, in the heart of the most prohunting country in the British Isles, the slogans on the T-shirts mock the slogans of the 'Animal Rights' protesters. They carry soft-porn messages, such as 'Don't Hump Foxes' with an illustration of a huntsman pressing himself against the brush of a fox.

Tim Morgan was very aggressive. It angered him that I was writing a book on fox-hunting. He thought the subject was far too narrow, and that the book should cover every aspect of human cruelty to animals. 'What are you going to do about cows?' he asked. 'What are you going to do about the way that they take the calves away from their mothers? Cows are very maternal creatures. Have you ever heard a cow moaning when they take away her young? Why don't you write about that?'

I told him that I felt it would be impossible to write a book that covered *every* aspect of the cruelty that human beings inflict on animals. The subject was so vast that the book would never be completed, and the idea of writing it was overwhelming. I thought of the unending research that would be necessary. I thought of the exhausting world-travel . . . What do they do to the emu in Australia? What do they do to the coyote in California?

Tim Morgan would accept no excuses. He became increasingly sarcastic and unpleasant. I finally asked why he didn't write the book himself. What was the point of attacking me because I couldn't tackle it? 'I have better things to do,' he snapped. I found this reply unanswerable.

'You don't eat meat, do you?' he suddenly asked me. His eyes had turned mustard yellow with hostility. 'I'm a half-vegetarian,' I said shiftly. I knew that he would be enraged by this idiotic answer, and that there could be no such creature as a half-vegetarian. But I had no wish to lie to him. A half-vegetarian was, more or less, exactly what I was.

He was predictably appalled by my confession. 'Do you really mean to say that you would eat a *slice of ham*?' His question had all the menace of the inquisition and made the practice of eating slices of ham sound intolerably filthy and barbaric.

I noticed that he was wearing rubber shoes because vegans consider it criminal to wear leather. I'd never much liked ham but I certainly couldn't pretend that I'd never tasted it. He made me feel so despicable about my ham-eating that I tried to hide my handbag. I realised to my horror that it had a leather strap.

When I visited this embattled little commune of vegans, I learned that they concern themselves only with 'Animal Rights'. They see their cause as quite separate from other causes which I would have thought were related.

'I've never been into Peace,' one of the girls said to me. 'Peace has never really interested me. Maybe I'm not really ready for it yet. I may get into it later.' She made 'Peace' sound like golf, a relaxing hobby that she might take up in her old age.

Tim Morgan said that he despised the League Against Cruel Sports. He found their approach much too moderate. 'If some bloody huntsman kills a fox – why shouldn't I kill him?' he asked me. It was the first time that I'd heard a young man openly advocating murder. But he didn't see his desire to commit murder as murderous. He felt he was only seeking justice.

While we were drinking soya milk coffee in one of the caravans, I became aware of persistent sobbing coming from a nearby stable. Tim Morgan didn't seem disturbed by it. The noise continued. It was similar to the crying of an infant, but it had a higher pitch.

I finally asked him to explain the disquieting sound. He said that it was a fox-cub which some woman had arrived with yesterday. She had saved it from a hunt after its mother had been killed. She had brought it up as a pet in London, but after a few months had decided that the little animal should be allowed to go back to the wild. Now she had brought it to his establishment to go through a process of rehabilitation.

I asked Tim Morgan what was going to happen to the young fox – how was he going to rehabilitate it? He said that he was going to let it spend the night in his stable and would then release it into the fields on the following day.

I asked him if there was much fox-hunting in the country that surrounded his sanctuary. Apparently there was a lot in the neighbourhood. 'Those bastards come right up here. They don't come on *my* land. They know better than to do that! But they hunt all through the woods up on the left.'

'But won't the fox-cub be eaten by the hounds?' I asked. Morgan shrugged. The hounds would probably get it. As it had been tamed it would not have learnt the various tricks of self-preservation that the wild fox-cub is taught by its mother. It would not have mastered the rudimentary rules of social fox behaviour. It might easily wander into the territory of another fox and that would be the end of it. As it had been used to having human-prepared meals of milk and tinned cat food, it would lack the ability to forage. If it managed to escape the hounds it would probably perish from starvation. Its prospects of survival were very slim. Tim Morgan accepted the unpromising future of the little fox with nonchalance.

He felt that a tamed wild animal was a creature that had been deprived of all its dignity. Its 'rights' had been violated. It would be better off meeting a violent but natural death than continuing in the disgrace of any further domesticity imposed by humans.

I wondered if the owner of the unhappy fox-cub had understood the attitudes of the commune when she brought in her pet for rehabilitation. It didn't seem to be getting much rehabilitation in this particular sanctuary. The animal was obviously terrified to find itself locked up in solitary confinement in a cold dark stable. It had suddenly been deprived of all the comforts and the affection it was used to receiving from its adopted human mother. The high-pitched sobbing coming from the stable was the sound of a creature traumatised by separation from everything it had learnt to depend on. Foxes in captivity tend to become over-attached to the human being that rears them. Much less independent than most dogs, they demand the continual presence of their love object and they manifest acute separation anxiety if their owner leaves them for a moment.

As the fox-cub was used to being treated as a household pet,

Tim Morgan could have taken it out of the stable and tried to comfort it; he could have seen if it was hungry or thirsty; the animal might have stopped that painful crying if he had allowed it to hear the sound of a human voice. But he refused to go near it for reasons of rigid principle. Now that it had entered his sanctuary, he was determined that it should have no further contact with any human being. If the abruptness of the transition that he'd imposed on the animal caused it distress, he was not concerned with that. Seeing himself as the defender of its 'rights', he was determined to sever its dependence on mankind and he was too intransigent a character to try to bring about a gradual severance.

Tim Morgan said that he was prepared to kill a huntsman because he hated the huntsman's cruelty to foxes, but the following morning he was going to take the fox-cub out of his stable and send it off to almost certain perdition. He seemed unable to identify with the plight of any individual animal. Although he fiercely denounced the wickedness of the fox-hunt because it allows the prey to experience an agony of prolonged terror even before the hounds reduce it to a bleeding pulp, the fox-cub that was howling in his sanctuary sounded just as frightened and tormented as the hunted foxes I'd heard screaming on the propaganda video film I'd been shown by the League Against Cruel Sports.

As I looked round the sanctuary, I felt that I was visiting a sanctuary for abstract 'Animal Liberation' principles rather than a haven for unlucky creatures. Even the turkeys and hens were depressed and depressing. They would never be roasted at Christmas but they looked ill-fed and mangy. There were a lot of stray dogs wandering around the muddy farmyard. Tim Morgan would not allow them to be destroyed, but they looked lost and neglected as if they were still straying. Neither he nor his long-haired girl assistants paid them any attention.

I was sorry for the naive woman who'd brought the vegan her cub for rehabilitation, and I felt certain that if she could have heard her pet crying so pitifully she would have instantly removed it from 'Little Heaven'. Morgan charged a fee when he rehabilitated foxes.

I was very glad to leave Tim Morgan's harsh sanctuary where the cries of the tormented fox-cub continued remorselessly, and I could understand why the League Against Cruel Sports is often discomfited by the attitudes and activities of its extremist fringe supporters. In 'Little Heaven' you had the impression that this particular 'Animal Rights' community was more obsessed with violent dislike of the human being than motivated by any strong love for animals.

# 5

# The Sport of Kings

*'Stags in the forest lie, hares in the valley-o,*
*Web-footed otters are spear'd in the lochs;*
*Beasts of the chase that are not worth a tally-ho;*
*All are surpass'd by the gorse-cover'd fox!'*

R. E. Egerton-Warburton

Hunting is regarded as an essentially old English tradition. As you travel round the British countryside it is interesting to see how many pubs are called the Golden Horn, the Horse and Hound, the Fox and Hare. The list is endless. Country hotels and restaurants are lavishly decorated with pictures of scarlet-coated men clearing a ditch or falling off at a fence. There are posters of hounds chasing a whisky bottle rather than a fox up a tree. Whips, spurs, saddles and horns are nailed up as ornaments on the walls.

Yet hunting for sport rather than food was originally a French tradition. Caius Julius Caesar noted, 'The Gauls coursed for sport rather than what they got.' The Anglo-Saxons hunted, but the object of their activities was to get meat for the pot and they were not interested in the elaborate trappings of 'the chase'. The ability to hunt was already the prerogative, if not the sport, of kings. As early as 1016 King Canute established the rules. 'It is my own wish that every man is to be entitled to his hunting in wood and field in his own land. But everyone is to avoid trespassing on my hunting wherever I wish to have it preserved, on pain of full fine.'

Earlier King Alfred was described as a 'keen huntsman', and his churchmen, from bishops down to lowly monks, also loved the sport, but hunting in England was not as ritualistic as in the French court. The Church had been granted large tracts of land by the King, so its servants were able to hunt from their monastic seclusion. By the eighth century the hunt was receiving much the same criticism that it receives now from the modern hunt saboteurs. Alcuin reprimanded the monks of Jarrow and Wearmouth. He urged them not to allow men under their supervision to dig out foxes or course hares. 'How wicked', he wrote, 'to leave the service of Christ for a fox-hunt.'

After 1066 William the Conqueror was depressed to find that British hunting was in a distressingly crude and disorganised state. He arranged his own hunts in the elegant Norman tradition, insisting that the hunters wear elaborate costumes similar to those worn by soldiers going into battle. The Conqueror brought to the hunt in England all the pomp, the pageantry, the discipline, the respect for horsemanship, courage and expertise that it still has today. He also introduced the horn. The French horn was to become an English symbol of sexual potency. The man with the horn – the 'horny' man – started to be admired and envied.

William also seized great tracts of forest as his preserves. Anyone who killed the King's game was blinded. The *Anglo-Saxon Chronicle* bemoaned the Norman King's strict laws:

*A hard man was the King*
*He was sunk in greed.*
*He set apart a vast deer*
*reserve and imposed laws*
*concerning it.*
*Whoever slew a hart or hind*
*was to be blinded*
*For he loved the stags as*
*dearly*

*As though he had been their father.*

The deer were loved like children by the King, but they were loved as his private quarry. The original meaning of the expression 'the quarry' described the ritual by which the stag was slaughtered. Having been shot with arrows it was then given the *coup de grâce* by the huntsman, who cut its throat with a knife. Once dead, the deer was elaborately carved up. Its testicles were removed, the first, and the most significant, part of the ceremony. After that, its right hoof was sliced off and given to the most important person present.

The fox is the inheritor of some of these ancient rituals. Its head and brush have become the prizes that the hunt distributes to important members of the field, while its 'pads' go to the hunting children.

Only the Norman barons originally hunted with the King; later with inter-marriage, some of the Anglo-Saxon gentry, the knights, bishops and abbots were occasionally allowed a 'chase'. As only nobles were permitted to hunt, the sport started to be seen as ennobling in itself. If anyone chased or killed a deer outside the confines of the established royal hunt he was not considered to be hunting, he was merely 'a poacher'. The same action was given a different name according to the class and wealth of the person doing it. A hunter had power, a non-hunter had none. Those who hunted game because they needed the food were seen as little better than animals. The 'chase' had become 'the occupation of the élite'.

'The passion for hunting is linked to excellence,' wrote M. Thiebaux in *The Medieval Chase*. 'Hunting had an ennobling effect upon its practitioners, and by the same token, adroitness in matters of the hunt was the mark of a noble person.'

Richard I brought in even severer penalties to protect the royal game. Offenders who killed a royal deer were not only blinded but also castrated. Barons and knights could escape these terrible punishments by paying the King to avoid them. Serfs were often executed.

Stag-hunting continued to be seen as the 'noblest' sport throughout the sixteenth and seventeenth centuries, and it flourished with the rise of the English squirearchy.

New forms of deer-hunting were introduced and it became a spectacle more than a chase. From the deer's viewpoint the rules were not very sporting. The stags were chased round enclosed parks, and the driven animals were either shot at by ladies and gentlemen with cross-bows or they were pursued by hounds, whose task was made much easier by the trail of blood streaming from the quarry's legs. Sometimes the tendons of the deer were slashed, sometimes one of their hooves was cut off.

Under the Tudors the English countryside was changed to accommodate the hunt. To make it more comfortable for hunters, woods were planted with gaps between the trees. The estates of the aristocracy were formally landscaped so that they were suitable for the hunt. There were masked hunts and fancy-dress hunts where the hunters dressed up in fanciful costumes, and often they were very drunk. Sometimes the prey was also dressed up and doomed stags went to their deaths with their antlers festooned with colourful ribbons. It was written of Henry VIII that as a young man he 'cared nothing but for girls and hunting'.

Elizabeth I enjoyed shooting driven deer and arranged to have an orchestra playing in the woods while she mowed them down. Her cross-bow would be passed to her by a servant dressed as a nymph. She once watched sixteen bucks being slaughtered by greyhounds as an after-dinner entertainment. She liked to cut the throat of the wounded animal herself. It is an unattractive image of Good Queen Bess, trifling with her sorbet, sipping her glass of Sauternes, and then administering so many *coups de grâce*.

James I used to dip his hands in the guts of murdered deer and daub his courtiers' faces with blood. Once a stag was disembowelled the ladies of his court would wash their hands in its gore, believing that it would whiten their skin.

The fox was also hunted, but only because it was seen as a verminous pest and a thief. It was not considered a noble animal, nor was it considered sport to chase one. A fox was destroyed rather than hunted, usually being driven to earth, dug out and then netted and beaten to death with clubs.

Under the Protectorship of Oliver Cromwell, hunting was disapproved of socially. The deer parks were broken up, and the sport of stag-hunting in England never really recovered. Hungry soldiers, disbanded after the Civil War, roamed the forests killing every animal they could find. The deer was threatened with extinction.

'Nothing remains', lamented a Cavalier, 'except rabbits and Roundheads.'

From the safe distance of the nineteenth century Macaulay mocked the attitude of the Puritans. He felt that they disliked all blood sports not because they cared about the pain inflicted on the animals, but because they hated the pleasure of the participants.

The Puritans certainly hated the drinking and revelry which have always been an essential accompaniment to hunting, but they also opposed the sport from a moral viewpoint. 'What Christian heart can take pleasure to see one poor beast to rend, tear, and kill another?' asked Philip Stubbs. 'I think it utterly unlawful, for any man to take pleasure in the pain and torture of any creature, or delight himself in the tyranny which the creatures exercise one over another or to make a recreation of their brutish cruelty which they practise one upon another,' wrote the strict Protestant, William Hinde.

After the Restoration, hunting regained its popularity. The hare replaced the deer as the favourite aristocratic quarry, but many young huntsmen found it could not provide the long fast 'runs' they liked to have. The hare meandered, it ran in circles and did not provide good sport.

Master's ancestor, the 5th Duke of Beaufort, discovered by

accident the pleasures of hunting the fox. After an unsatisfactory day out hunting hares, his hounds found a fox in a wood and he decided to encourage them to chase it. He and his followers then enjoyed one of the longest 'runs' of their lives, and the Duke realised how superior the fox was to the hare as a prey. The Dukes of Monmouth, Buckingham and Grafton also started to hunt foxes and other noblemen copied them. The 2nd Duke of Buckingham became the first noble casualty of the new sport. On a freezing evening he waited interminably for a fox to be dug out of the hole where it had gone to ground, and died of a fever as he waited.

As the aristocrats owned vast tracts of land, the areas where they hunted the fox came to be known by the names of their packs of hounds as if they were actual geographical locations. In the nineteenth century, if a fox-hunter lived in, say, Leicestershire, and was asked where he came from, he would reply that he was from the Quorn or the Pytchley. The name of the pack of hounds that a person supported was seen as far more important than the town or the county from which he originally came.

The areas of land over which the different hunts hunted were enormous. Lord Berkeley's hunt stretched from Bristol to Kensington Gardens, Sir Richard Puleston's from Flintshire to Leicestershire, and Lord Darlington's hunt from Durham to Doncaster. The Dukes of Grafton had a hunting empire covering Surrey, Norfolk and Northamptonshire. The 2nd Duke of Grafton was responsible for building London Bridge. He found the Croydon ferry maddeningly slow and it ruined his 'runs'. His hounds had to be ferried over first and the followers then had to wait for the boat to return, which he found both disruptive and unsatisfactory. For this reason he arranged for a Bill to be passed through Parliament so that his hunt could follow an alternative and superior route. It is strange to think that foxes were once hunted and killed in Eaton Square.

In the London Borough of Islington, the council has

recently taken a very anachronistic step – it has banned all fox-hunting in the borough despite the fact that mothers complain that there is not a blade of grass on which their children can play. It will be curious to see if New Yorkers soon follow suit and pass a law to ban both fox- and bear-hunting in Brooklyn and the Bronx.

Islington Council could be accused of 'shutting the stable door after the steed and the hunter have flown', but the fears that led them to take this ludicrously unnecessary legal precaution are still interesting. Do many Londoners have an atavistic terror that at any moment they may hear the dreaded cry of 'Tally Ho'? Do they really expect to see a pack of hounds in full cry with some whip-cracking huntsman and a great stream of mounted followers creating havoc in the city's congested traffic as they gallop down the tarmac ignoring every red traffic-light and zebra crossing?

If this dreaded hunt were to take place, it would be interesting to examine the state of the horses' legs. The foxes killed presumably would be few and the fox-hunters would undoubtedly have a 'rotten day', but it would make a beautiful hunting scene. It is regrettable that this strict new urban law now makes it one that Londoners will never witness.

# 6

# Hazards of the Chase

*'Just enough danger to make sport delightful,*
*Toil just sufficient to make slumber sweet.'*
R. E. Egerton-Warburton

Fox-hunting is the most dangerous of all sports. More people are brain-damaged, paralysed, blinded, disfigured and killed while fox-hunting than pursuing any other perilous or unnecessary activity – skiing, boxing or motor-bike racing, for example. The range of possible accidents offered by the hunt is enormous. The unpredictable behaviour of other horses and riders, the rabbit hole, the hidden tree stump, the wire in the fence, the treacherous patches of bog, all can produce fatalities. The very code and etiquette of the fox-hunter puts him or her in danger. The rules ask for more stoicism than is ever demanded by the military. The discipline is much fiercer. If riders fall and sustain injury they are not meant to let it be known that they are hurt, for then the other members of the hunt will have to attend to them and it will spoil the 'run'. Whereas a soldier is permitted to announce that he has been hit by a bullet, a fallen fox-hunter suffering from multiple fractures is meant to announce that he or she feels perfectly all right.

A second rule of etiquette also creates unnecessary casualties. The fallen rider should never let go of the reins. The hunt does not enjoy having a riderless horse galloping in its midst. The horse has to be caught before it causes another accident and this again ruins the run. This rule of the rein is so ingrained that it becomes for the good huntsman an automatic response, and many riders are dragged horribly after a fall which can sometimes bring down the horse on top of them, so they are crushed under its weight or kicked in the face.

I spoke to a girl who'd had all the bones of her chest smashed to splinters because she would not let go of the reins. 'I still remember trying to cling on to those reins. I was clinging and clinging to them and then the horse came crashing down and everything went black as I was knocked unconscious. I'd have been fine if I'd just let go of them, but I'd have died rather than do that. The rules of the hunt were much more than rules. They were one's morality.'

The same morality was described by Nimrod, the great Victorian chronicler of the fox-hunt. Writing in 1822, he gave an account of a day with the Quorn:

> Two horses are seen loose in the distance – a report is flying about that one of the field is badly hurt, and something is heard of a collar-bone being broken, others say it is a leg: but the pace is too good to enquire. A cracking of rails is now heard, and one gentleman's horse is to be seen resting, neatly balanced, across one of them, his rider being on his back in the ditch, which is on the landing side. It is evidently a case of peril, but *the pace is too good* to afford help.

Nimrod continues in this same breezy vein and ends up with a nice little fragment of hunt dialogue:

> 'Who is that under his horse in the brook?'
>
> 'Only Dick Christian,' answers Lord Forester, 'and it's nothing new to him.'
>
> 'But he'll be drowned,' exclaims Lord Kinnaird.
>
> 'I shouldn't wonder,' observes Mr William Coke. 'But the *pace is too good* to enquire.'

'Cases of peril' have never received much sympathy or help on the hunting field. Husbands see their wives and children go crashing down and 'cast a cold eye'. Wives see their husbands and children turn fearful somersaults, but leave them lying in appallingly vulnerable situations, at risk of being trampled to mincemeat by the herd of oncoming hooves.

'Are you all right, darling?' The question is shouted over the shoulder to the fallen. But the hooves behind them are thundering. The hounds are giving out their beautiful haunting wail. The noise of the huntsman's horn is floating through the countryside, with its unique and challenging music. The hunters are drunk with 'the pace' and the danger. 'Darling' may be all right. 'Darling' may be far from all right. The riders make the polite enquiry, but as the question is shouted over the shoulder, the shout can get lost in the wind. They don't always stop. On the 'field' they can behave like mounted Pharisees and go galloping on. Ties of blood and friendship lose all meaning in the chase.

Having given no quarter to other victims, the hunters ask none for themselves. They know that if their necks are fatally broken, the nearest five-bar gate will be ceremonially removed from its hinges for field hands and farm boys to use as a stretcher. They will be carried in state to the nearest Land Rover. 'He went the way he would have wanted to go,' the hunt will say philosophically as it meets to drink port in the evening. This will not necessarily be a facile or callous response. Many fox-hunters have announced their desire to die in, or from, the saddle. The Labour peer, Lord Paget, has always expressed a longing to be killed out hunting as his father was before him.

When a keen fox-hunter hears that a friend has been stricken by cancer or some other fatal disease he finds it tragic for different reasons to those of the non-hunting layman. 'It's so dreadfully sad that he wasn't killed out hunting. It would have been so much better for him. That way he would have died doing the only thing he wanted to do.'

Lord Longford, the writer and prison visitor, is the son of a Master of Fox-hounds. He told me that his father had taken his hunting very seriously. 'My father wanted to be killed in a cavalry charge even more than he wanted to be killed out hunting. But I suppose it's really all the same thing. In fact my father was killed in a fusiliers' charge . . . He more or less got what he wanted . . .'

Lord Longford described a very frightening hunting experience which he had had two years before. He was staying in a house-party in Ireland and was reading about some hunt in the Irish newspapers. He made the foolish mistake of saying that he would give anything for a day with the hounds. 'I only said it out of bravado. I was saying what my father would have liked me to have said. I didn't mean it at all.'

The other guests in the house-party instantly took up his idle remark. He learned to his horror that a meet was taking place on the following day. He tried to get out of it by saying that he hadn't got a horse. That didn't work – they could find him one. He said that he had no hunting clothes. Hunting clothes were immediately produced.

He was then seventy-eight, and had not ridden for forty years. He found himself setting off to the meet on a spirited Arab stallion. 'I went out hunting out of cowardice rather than courage. I kept thinking about my Master of Fox-hounds father and I was more frightened of arousing contempt than I was frightened of the horrible frisky Arab.'

As Lord Longford set off, a groom warned him that his horse hated water, which alarmed him still further because the Irish countryside is crossed by so many ditches. By ill luck the very first jump that he came to was water – a deep and treacherous-looking river. The Arab refused and Lord Longford was secretly delighted. If the horse wouldn't go over water, he would have to accept it. He felt he'd had a miraculous escape. He'd been given a way out of this terrifying hunt and could go home with dignity, his courage unquestioned. Just as he thought he was saved, the Arab changed its mind. It no longer hated water, for no apparent reason it suddenly loved it. It jumped the water, leaving Lord Longford flat on his back on the ground on the near side.

'Everyone got very excited about my toss,' he said. 'Hunting people love you to have a toss. Isn't it funny how much they love it? People kept galloping up to me and telling me that I felt great. "You feel really great, don't you?" they kept saying. I didn't feel in the least great. I'd just had an awful fall and I was only grateful that I wasn't dead. But everyone seemed to think that I felt *better* than I'd felt before my toss. I found that very peculiar.'

His horse was caught for him. He remounted and continued his miserable chase. The Irish pack had a woman as its master. She was the next to have a frightful fall. She came down in a lane and was very badly injured. Lord Longford used the excuse to dismount and get her on to a five-bar gate. He carried her into an ambulance in which she was then taken off to hospital. He thought that now that the master had been removed with critical injuries the hunt would come to an end and his miseries would cease. But not at all. Someone else took over the mastership and the hunt went on.

'I couldn't believe it,' he said. 'The master's demise didn't faze them at all. I had to go on to the kill. And all the time I was remembering what a high percentage of people in wheelchairs we have in the House of Lords, and nearly all of them hunting victims. Hunting is such a strange business – I wonder whether it's more valuable to spend every minute of the day following the hounds like my father did, or to spend one's time talking to child murderers like Myra Hindley, and Ian Brady, like I do. My father's life was certainly more healthy and active – I just sit around in their cells.'

The hunting community's fatalistic attitude towards death and injury has always baffled those who cannot share it. Talking to members of the hard-riding Leicestershire set, I was surprised how calmly they accepted the fact that Prince Charles has a very good chance of perishing on the hunting field. They say that his life is never in greater danger than when he is following the hounds. His security men cannot ride beside him as they are not trained to ride over the enormous Leicestershire jumps. They can only follow him in vehicles on the roads.

The Prince has described some of the hazards to which he is exposed once he takes to the chase. 'The magic in Leicestershire is still there, although I must admit that it takes a little time to appreciate it when you first go to the Quorn or the Belvoir. The great Duke of Wellington apparently used to encourage as many of his cavalry officers as possible to hunt in the Shires in order that they could acquire that particular brand of dash, fire and an eye for country which so distinguished the British cavalry in the eighteenth and nineteenth centuries. When you first visit the Quorn you can't help feeling, while being trampled in the rush, that the majority of the field are still in training for one of Wellington's campaigns!'

The royal security men with their superb and sophisticated training and all their modern weaponry become pathetically useless figures once the Prince enters something that closely resembles 'one of Wellington's cavalry charges'. If he is 'trampled in the rush', they can only bemoan the fact sitting in some lane in their high-security vans.

The Prince is completely on his own once he is riding over the taxing country of the Shires and, as one who has been deprived by birth of one of the most important human luxuries – privacy, he probably feels a heady sense of freedom as he escapes the tyranny of constant surveillance by bodyguards. He can forget about his royal duties. He can forget about his beautiful wife's mega-star image. He can feel a fresh wind blowing in his face.

On the hunting field he is at risk from the extremist hunt saboteurs, who loathe the idea of their future King hunting; he is also at the mercy of his usual enemies, such as members of the IRA. The hunting set accept the fact that he's in serious danger with a fatalistic shrug. If something happens to him, well he will have a princely end. No other end can be better than that.

As a child I remember being told about the macabre fate of a quiet, friendless little maiden lady who lived near Dublin. She was a solitary huntswoman. Although she had hunted six days a week for most of her life, she had not established any social contact with her fellow huntsmen, but they still respected her for her horsemanship and her expertise. One morning she rose early as had been her life-long custom and as usual spent the day hunting with the Kildare hounds. Her fellow riders noted that she 'went particularly well' and she was 'in at the kill'. She said goodnight to the master and set off in the dusk to hack her exhausted mare back home. She eventually came to a bridge, where she dismounted. She covered her horse with a rug as it was still sweating and she was obviously anxious not to let it get a chill. She tied it up to a tree with a halter so that it would not come to any harm. She then climbed on to the parapet of the bridge, hurled herself into the river, and was drowned within a few minutes. Her body was recovered after her bowler hat was seen bobbing towards a weir as it went floating down the torrent.

At the time her story haunted me, and I found it impossible to understand how this lonely little woman managed to feel in the mood to go out hunting if she had decided to end her life. Her suicide appeared to be coolly premeditated because it was abnormal for her to have brought a halter and a horse rug to the meet. Only now do I wonder if she, too, had the curious dream of dying with the hunt and, not feeling that she was morally entitled to risk the life of her mare by riding irresponsibly, she saw her chosen final solution as the next best thing to the perfect death that she craved. She'd seen to it that she had a 'good day' on her very last day on earth and, with the unsentimental purposefulness of every dedicated hunter, she'd quietly gone from 'a view' to a death in the evening.

Opponents of fox-hunting see the hunting enthusiasts' disregard for their safety as part of their passion for blood sacrifice rather than valour. Their courage is dismissed as idiocy and lack of imagination. 'As they seem too stupid to recognise the risks that they are taking, I can't respect them for their bravery,' a passionate enemy of animal blood sports said to me. 'Fox-hunters are like old generals. They don't die . . . Well, they don't die as much as they sometimes pretend to. But they certainly fade away and I'll tell you where they fade to . . . They fade to Stoke Manderville and similar institutions for paraplegics. But they don't like to admit that . . . Somehow it doesn't really have the red-coated glory that the silly idiots love so much.'

# 7

# The Quarry

*'Believe me, it is not pleasant getting up at five o'clock every morning for a couple of months or so in the autumn which is the time we go cub-hunting, when the young hounds get an opportunity to learn what it's all about, and so do the foxes.'*

Henry, 10th Duke of Beaufort

The rich are different, claimed Scott Fitzgerald, and if he had moved in English fox-hunting circles he might have had to say that the rich who fox-hunt are different from those who don't.

*They say that even up in heaven the rich lie late and snore*
*While the poor man rises at seven to do the celestial chore.*

So goes the old anonymous folksong. This accusation could hardly be levelled at the rich fox-hunters. However late they have been out drinking, however severe the hangover, the dedicated huntsman rises much earlier than the poor man of the song. He is the servant of the 'scent', on which his whole way of life depends.

The ideal scent conditions for hunting are at night, which is why wolf packs have always hunted then. In Great Britain the wolf has been exterminated by man, who has then copied his role and become the fox's most deadly predator. The fox-hunter sees himself as restoring nature's ecological balance. The human fox-hunter has been forced to adapt his hunting times for obvious reasons, but he still allows himself far less sleep than the poor man in the ballad. John Peel was certainly not 'kenned' lying late, and snoring. He was 'kenned' at the break of day. Hunters of fox-cubs are particularly disciplined and get up at four in the morning.

The fox-hunting mystique about 'scent' goes back to the nineteenth century and before. William Somerville, the Regency poet and Master of Fox-hounds, wrote:

*To every shrub the warm effluvia cling,*
*Hang on the grass, impregnate earth and skies.*
*With nostril opening wide, o'er hill, o'er dale,*
*The vigorous hounds pursue, with every breath*
*Inhale the grateful steam . . .*

When Somerville makes his steam 'grateful', his pathetic fallacy illustrates the passionate gratitude that fox-hunters feel whenever conditions produce a good 'scent'. Experienced fox-hunters claim to be able to prophesy the scent conditions that will prevail during the day when they stick their heads out through their windows on awakening.

In one sense the fox owes its life to its scent. The dog fox attracts and finds his vixen mate by leaving scented love messages in strategic places around the countryside. When the fox-cub gets separated from its mother, it finds her through her scent. The fox, then, often perishes as a result of the same scent which first gave it life and helped to preserve it.

The fox gives out scent from three different parts of its body: from its brush, its anus and its pads. The scent lands on the soil in little bubbles resembling tiny dewdrops, which then rise with the vapour from the earth and dissolve when they meet the air. Ideally, the earth should be warmer than the air to produce a good scent for the hounds. Snow is therefore 'good', whereas frost is very 'bad' indeed.

In 1915, the childhood friend of Siegfried Sassoon, known as Stephen in the poet's fictionalised memoirs, wrote to him and described his reaction to all the horror and carnage of warfare in the trenches. The young man complained that there was not a 'jumpable' fence in Flanders, and said that he felt 'just about as bucked as I should be if I was booked for a week with the Pytchley and it froze the whole time'. Stephen was killed shortly after writing this letter, which gives some indication of the intense dread of frost that the fox-hunter still feels.

Ploughed land, known as 'plough', is also loathed by the hunt, for not only is it much colder than grass, but it also has a very strong odour of its own which masks the scent. 'Plough' has other disadvantages which also make it anathema to the fox-hunter. Modern, sophisticated machines dig very deep furrows, which make exhausting ground for both horses and hounds to cover. Ploughed earth sticks to the pads of the fox, preventing any droplets of its odour from falling on the soil. Keen fox-hunters shudder on hearing the word 'plough', just as other people recoil at the mention of some dread disease.

Because of the golden rule that the soil should always be warmer than the air to produce a 'good scent', hunters of fox-cubs rise especially early. The cub-hunting season is in September and October because the weather tends to be warm at that time of year, so the hunters struggle up in the cold and the dark to catch the last of the night air before the sun removes its chill.

Scientists and fox-hunting experts have written extensively about all the niceties of 'scent' and the infinite number of factors which affect it. They have not always agreed on the conditions that would produce the perfect scent from the huntsman's point of view, but they all agree that high winds and cattle, sheep, and obviously frost and 'plough' are highly undesirable, while quibbling about the degree to which fertilisers, manure, chemical sprays and exhaust fumes inflict lethal damage on the 'scent'. Henry Beaufort always had something revealing to say about every aspect of his favourite sport.

'There is nothing as mysterious as scent – except women' was his last word on the subject.

The current passion for car-hunting has created a new hazard for the embattled traditional hunt. Fifty thousand people in Great Britain now follow the packs in vehicles, and many of them car-hunt as often as four days a week, which demonstrates the measure of their keenness. These sedentary yet ardent hunt supporters bring with their passion and dedication to the Sport of Kings all the disadvantages and the pollution of their fumes.

The modern fox, with its notorious cunning, now often outfoxes pursuers by deliberately running through the traffic, knowing that its delicate aroma will be completely eradicated by the noxious exhaust fumes of diesel engines, jeeps, Rolls-Royces and farm trucks.

When the steam engine was first invented, the hunt went into metaphorical mourning and prophesied the end of the British way of life and the extinction of the fox-hunt. The sport has had much more 'staying power' than was ever imagined, although it now has to contend with far greater threats than any the old hunting pessimists possibly could have envisaged.

Anyone who breaks the scent is seen as committing a criminal act by the purist fox-hunter. He regards such an act with the same horror that boxing fans might feel if ardent supporters of the sport rushed into the ring with clubs and broke the fighters' legs.

But the modern packs have had to compromise and accommodate themselves to a mechanised era which has no recognition of the subtleties of their age-old codes. Warts and all, car-hunters have to be tolerated, for they pay their subscriptions to the hunt and, as fox-hunting is now an immensely expensive pastime, their support has been increasingly necessary in a period of galloping inflation. They are an important means of ensuring the survival of this archaic sport.

Ulrica Murray Smith was joint master of the Quorn for

more than twenty years, and is the author of an informative book called *The Magic of the Quorn*, which has a eulogistic preface written by Prince Charles. Ulrica cuts through all the mystique and fuss about 'scent' in a fashion that is refreshing and unexpected coming from a fox-hunting devotee. 'What conditions are required for scent to be good has been argued and written about *ad infinitum*,' she writes. 'But it does seem to be obvious that some foxes smell more than others. This, after all, applies to people too!'

Ulrica Murray Smith is not only very 'sound' about 'scent', but she also gives a vivid description of the fox-hunter's pride and delight in his wounds. 'When Alan Whicker was making a film of the Quorn he told me afterwards that he could not see that it was cruel to the fox, but he did think that it was terribly cruel to the people who rode to hounds. "Leicestershire seemed to echo with the dull crack of breaking bones."

'I have broken quite a few myself, and came to know the paybed wing at the Nottingham General Hospital rather too well, at one time . . .

'On one occasion when there was boggy ground in front of some rails, my animal failed to get her feet out to take off, falling and then treading all over me getting up, and so breaking my leg.'

Ulrica was saved by the late Duke of Beaufort, who had broken his leg the year before. He had constructed a giant stirrup which could contain his plaster, and this had enabled him to continue to hunt. Master lent this monstrous stirrup to Ulrica and she was also able to go hunting in what she calls 'comparative comfort'. Her hardy attitude enabled her to surmount other vicissitudes.

'I broke vertebrae twice. The first time I wore a sort of plaster barrel round my middle, which entailed buying a maternity dress to cover it, and which does nothing for one's morale. The second time the break was between my shoulder blades, so plaster was out of the question and I just lived on dope. Fortunately, at this time I had the most wonderful old horse, given to me by Terry Skinner, called Top Brass, who was an absolute patent safety. So I was able to go out hunting on him for an hour or so, fortified by masses of pain killers swallowed down with neat whisky. It was better than staying at home!

'I am always frightfully disagreeable when in hospital so that my friends dread coming to see me. When she broke her neck, Maggy Myddleton was simply wonderful – she was so cheerful. She sat bolt upright, looking rather like Buddha, with a crown over her head, with steel rods from it literally driven into her head, holding it absolutely fixed to the plaster below. I found it incomprehensible how cheerful she was, in that awful position.

'Maggy has sadly since her accident had to give up hunting with us, but Rid, her husband, still comes all the way from Chirk Castle in Wales, to hunt on Mondays . . .

'Riding in an Oxford Grind some twenty-five years ago Mike Crawshaw had the most terrible fall, which left him completely paralysed from the waist down. Despite this he does much work in the county, sits in the House of Lords, helps with Riding for the Disabled and other charities. He shoots from a Land Rover, and he comes out hunting using a special saddle, but dressed in proper hunting clothes, scarlet coat and all. He has no feeling in his legs, so a few months ago when he had a fall from his horse, he broke his leg, without knowing it; now his leg has set itself crooked.'

# 8

# The Fox-Hound

*'How they drive to the front! How they bustle and spread! Those badger-pied beauties that open the ball!'*

Whyte Melville to the 9th Duke of Beaufort

A hound starts its life as 'a whelp'. Its dew claws are removed, its nails are pared and it is worm-dosed. It is named at birth. Its name, like that of all its brothers and sisters in the same litter, starts with the same initial as its mother's name. It is then put out at 'walk', which means it is adopted by a farmer or some other figure paid by the hunt to exercise and feed it.

In its period of fosterhood the hound goes through its first process of being 'entered', which means it receives its first lessons on how to be a hunter of foxes. It is taught the dangers of traffic, and trained to understand that chasing chickens and sheep is an anti-social activity. Separated from its family, it is meant to become a resourceful individual. Like all foster children and children sent early to boarding school, there is always a risk that its foster parents may exploit and neglect it.

There is a danger that those who accept a hound 'at walk' can take the hunt's money and make a mean little profit by under-feeding and under-exercising the puppy entrusted to their care. They can also go to the other extreme and treat it as such a beloved household pet that they make it too indolent and domestic ever to take its place in the pack as a courageous and fierce fox-hound.

After a few months of being 'at walk', the whelp is returned to the hunt, where it then lives 'on the flags' or in the kennels. It is fed on 'pudding' or meal porridge and in the summer months before the hunting season starts it is entered in the local puppy show. The hunt offers prizes for the best 'young entry' and these puppy shows are vitally important.

The whole future and existence of the fox-hunt as a sport depends on the goodwill of the local farmers. The veteran fox-hunter, Colonel John Cook, in his book *Observations on Fox-hunting*, made a plea to potential masters. 'You should endeavour to gain the goodwill of the farmers,' he wrote, 'for if any respectable body of persons suffer from hunting it is them. And I think it is not only ungentlemanly but impolitic to treat them in the field or elsewhere otherwise than with kindness and civility.'

It is the farmers who take in the majority of the young hounds 'at walk', and the puppy show as a local event has been created to involve the farmer and reward him for his contribution to the hunt. It is not always a pleasant experience to be entrusted with the care of a wild young hound. A whelp can cause havoc in a household by chewing up shoes and cushions. It can attack the beloved family cat, kill the dogs, maul the chickens and chase the pregnant ewes. A pedigree hound is a very valuable animal and those who have it 'at walk' take on the worry and responsibility of seeing to its safety. A whelp has to be constantly supervised and requires a lot of exercise.

The role of those who take on the task of fostering the young hounds is one of altruism – and self-sacrifice. They look after a puppy when it is still untrained in traffic and undisciplined, and at the most difficult and destructive stage of its life. They never get the satisfaction of seeing it become a docile and affectionate pet.

The puppy show, with prizes offered by the hunt, gives the walkers the fun and the opportunity of competing with other walkers and, if the puppy they have unselfishly nurtured wins, they have the excitement of sharing its glory and its prize.

Having cared for the hound from babyhood, the farmers continue to feel affection for Venus or Bellboy once they join the pack, and watch their individual progress through the hunting season with a special interest. This personal involvement makes the farmers put up more easily with the inconvenience and damage that they suffer yearly from the activities of the hunt.

Once the young hound is removed from the care of the fostering farmers and is taken back by the hunt, it starts the equivalent of military training: it is very seriously 'entered to fox'. It has to learn its name and is taught to understand the meaning of 'Ware wing', 'Ware hare' and 'Ware wire', which mean respectively don't chase birds or hares, and look out for hidden barbed wire. At this stage of its career a hound is often severely 'rated', which means it is cursed and punished and struck by a whip.

The most serious crime that a fox-hound can commit is 'to run riot', or in simpler words to chase any bird or animal that is not a fox. Pheasants, deer, sheep, cows and ordinary dogs all present temptations, and huntsmen have to find a balance by which they make it immune to such temptations from fear of chastisement without ruining its future as a fox-hunter. If a hound is too severely 'rated' its heart can be broken and it is no longer a useful member of the pack.

In the United States in the hunting counties many of the forests have been stocked with white-tailed deer by the game commissions. The American huntsmen have a more severe problem training their young fox-hounds to 'be steady' to stags and to ignore them than most of their English counterparts. They use artificial deer scent to tempt the young hounds and then chastise them for following it. They keep a ferocious buck in the kennels so that the whelps develop a fear of stags after they have received one or two wounds from an antler. The whippers-in are not only supplied with a whip during the period when the hounds are being 'entered' – they also carry 22 calibre pistols loaded with bird shot, so that, like Pavlov's dog, when the hounds commit a misdemeanour they receive a sharp shock and are peppered with small stinging bullets. 'What a delightful way to train a young dog,' a hunting anti said to me.

Hounds are never counted in a normal fashion by the hunt. They are counted only in couples. A pack is made up of sixteen and a half couples of hounds, which sounds alarming to anyone unfamiliar with the hunting vocabulary.

In the important weeks before the cub-hunting season opens, the young hounds are taken out by the huntsman, dressed in his hunt coat and bowler. They are coupled with an older and experienced hound so that they can learn the techniques of scrambling through a thicket of thorns or a fence of barbed wire with the minimum physical harm. They also receive a few kicks so that they learn one of the most essential lessons of their profession: to beware of horses' hooves. The huntsman watches the traits in their character very carefully at this juncture. He looks for defects which will disqualify a hound from becoming an honourable member of the pack. A hound which is a 'babbler' is regarded with disapproval and dismay. Such a hound gives cry before it has picked up a scent and confuses both the field and its fellow hounds. It is as unpopular as a human being who refuses to stop talking although he has nothing interesting to say.

A 'mute' hound is also very undesirable. It picks up a scent and keeps the secret to itself, never giving tongue at all. It is seen as a spoilsport and 'mute' hounds are soon kicked out of the pack. Other undesirables are 'tail' hounds which lag behind the other dogs, and 'skirters' which cut corners and prefer to do a little private hunting on their own. Certain hounds never learn to acquire a taste for hunting. Like Ferdinand the Bull, they have no desire to provide a spectacle. Ferdinand had a happy ending because he existed only as a character in a fairy-tale. Any hound who takes a pacifist attitude is shot without compunction.

Whenever some unfortunate hound is thrown out of the

pack, in hunt language, it is 'drafted'. When young Americans were 'drafted' in the Vietnam War, they were forcibly introduced into the fighting pack. Their situation was the very opposite to the 'drafted' hound, which is dismissed in disgrace and condemned to death as being unfit to fight with its peers.

The month of September is the most important in the life of a young 'undrafted' fox-hound. 'In September it is still light before six,' writes J. N. P. Watson, lifelong fox-hunter and correspondent for *Country Life*. 'We set out in the dark.' He then corrects his own 'we'. He points out that hunt subscribers have no prerogative to hunt fox-cubs, and goes on to express his worship of the whole hunting hierarchy in the following sonorous little sentences. 'That is the master's perquisite. And his alone.'

Watson then waxes lyrical. 'But those who favour the still of an autumn daybreak, the early morning smells, the birdsong and the golden tints, and who cannot do with too much of the atmosphere of fox-hunting will doubtless telephone the master to attend.'

Like many other writers about fox-hunting, Watson makes the whole enterprise seem a little more glorious than any outsider or non-enthusiast of the sport can find it. His 'golden tints' and his 'birdsong' all sound so pure and delightful. They cast a beautiful and roseate glow over an act of calculated cruelty. When Watson's cub-hunters set off bravely in the dark, they have an unpleasant aim in mind. They plan to slaughter a defenceless animal and its young. If a gang of delinquent boys were to murder a cat with its kittens, the British public would be disgusted. Few people would be impressed by the fact that they had set off 'in the dark' in order to do it. The brutality of their act would not be made more palatable because it was committed while the lark was singing and dawn was turning the sky to gold. But the fox-hunter feels that he is exonerated by the beauty of nature as he teaches his young hounds to acquire a taste for fox-blood. 'If a young hound is to be encouraged,' writes Watson, 'he must have blood.'

In general, the fox-hunter is fairly honest about his requirements and shows little hypocrisy. Like a young hound, he must have blood and he doesn't mind saying so. Since so many people now oppose the sport, he sometimes goes in for cant about the huntsman's 'duty' to the farmer. But usually he states his attitudes fairly honestly. The poet Will H. Ogilvie neatly expressed the fox-hunter's attitude:

*He holds no brief for slaughter, but the cubs must take their chance*
*The weak must first go under that the strong may lead the dance;*
*And when the grey strides out and shakes the foam-flecks from his rings*
*The happiest man in England would not change his place with kings.*

Many British animal lovers loathe the truthful and naive exuberance of this kind of lyric. Their blood boils when they are presented with such a disarming and jaunty piece of philosophy. They loathe the whole celebration of the weak going under, and detest the assumption that the defenceless always ought to be sacrificed so that the strong can 'lead the dance'.

When the huntsman slaughters the vixen he is ensuring that he will have future sport in two different ways, both of which are unacceptable to the anti's, the different groups who would like the sport to be made illegal. The murder of the vixen gives the hounds a taste for blood, and while some of the cubs are torn apart a few are spared, not out of pity or mercy, but to ensure that they become good 'quarry' for the future. The experience of seeing their mother murdered underground is meant to traumatise the cubs, so that they feel there is no safety in going to earth. This makes them tend to run above ground when they are hunted in future seasons and the hunters are given better sport and better runs.

Once the young hounds have obeyed the instruction, 'Go in

and tear him,' the master and the other hunt followers make a great fuss of them and they are rewarded and praised. All this encouragement makes them understand what humans require of them. By nature hounds have no interest in hunting the fox, they have to be indoctrinated before they learn to lust for his blood.

Like boxers and runners, the professional life of a fox-hound is a short one. In a seven-month hunting season it walks about thirty miles to the meet many days a week. It does another twenty-five miles once it starts chasing foxes in earnest, and then has to jog yet another thirty miles to get back to the kennels. The life is exhausting and very few hounds last more than five seasons. They sustain horrible injuries scrambling through barbed wire fences and other obstacles. They are trampled by the horses of bad riders. When the hunt is in full cry they may find themselves separated from the pack and be discovered wandering unattended on main roads where they can be run over by vehicles.

In the old days of the steam engine clever foxes were reputed to lead the hounds down to the railway tracks just when the train was coming. The modern fox has no need of such calculated timing. It only has to lead the dogs over a busy road, where they will be struck by some hunting enthusiast hollering and racing on his motor-bike.

But those are just the risks of the game. And even if the hound avoids all these hazards it is doomed to die an untimely and unnatural death.

The moment that a hound becomes worn out and proves unsatisfactory to the hunt it is shot. Sixteen thousand hounds are destroyed regularly in Great Britain each year. This statistic includes stag-hounds and beagles, amongst others. But it is still a large figure. The loyalty between gallant master and his trusty hound exists only in legend and literature. Masters of Fox-hounds have been known to bemoan a 'bad' season when they've killed far more hounds than they've killed foxes.

# 9

# The Language of the Hunt

*'What so wild as words are?'*

Browning

Few things to do with the fox-hunt are called what one would expect them to be. Some of the oddities of hunting terminology are well known. Hounds do not have noses and paws and tails, they have 'muzzles' and 'pads' and 'sterns' like ships. Other examples of fox-hunting idiom are more confusing and provide great possibilities for the solecism. Hounds do not smell the scent of a fox, they 'wind' it. And although they don't have noses, they have the perverse ability to 'nose' it. Hounds never bark, they bay and 'speak' like humans. They also 'throw tongue' and 'make music'. When they 'run heel', they are not underfoot as one might expect, they are running in the opposite direction to which the fox is heading. When they 'mark' a fox, they don't leave their teeth marks in it, they surround the drain or the burrow where it has taken cover. When they 'chop' a fox they are not behaving like Lizzie Borden with her axe, but they surprise the animal when it is sleeping.

Just as the fox-hound has no paws in the language of the hunt neither does its quarry. The traditional practice of cutting off the pads of the dead fox and giving them like a medal to children who manage to be in at the kill would perhaps be more disquieting if these children were given bleeding paws. 'I remember my nursery was always full of bits of fox,' the daughter of a Master of Fox-hounds said to me.

A fox has a mask and no head, a brush, and no tail. When it defecates, it makes 'billetts'. A huntsman wishing to insult another huntsman would be ill-advised to describe his enemy as a 'bloody billett'.

When a fox leaves a trail of scent it leaves a 'line', and anything that obliterates this line 'foils' it. The fox goes to ground in 'an earth' rather than a hole. The huntsman also has private terms for his activities. He 'draws' a 'covert' when searching small areas of scrub and gorse and woodland for a fox. He chooses the 'day's draw' when he selects the area of countryside where he plans to hunt and sees that any earths where the fox might take refuge are blocked by human earth-stoppers with spades. He 'casts' like a fisherman when he helps the hounds to recover a lost 'line'. He gives a high hunting scream on seeing a fox from afar: this is a 'view halloa', pronounced holler. His followers pick up his half-scream, half-shout, with the echo of 'Huic halloa'. When the huntsman 'lifts' his hounds he doesn't gather them up in his arms, he keeps them in an area where a fox has been viewed.

He curses and shouts 'Hold hard' when riders come dangerously close to his hounds. His most important cry is, 'Go in and tear him!' This is the famous old cry of the kill, by which he instructs his hounds to rip the fox apart. Animal protesters have taped many of these cries and they replay the tapes in their homes with revulsion. Siegfried Sassoon recalled visiting an elderly military gentleman who loved the cry so much that he had taught his parrot to repeat it incessantly. Not everyone would relish the sound of a bird squawking these hunting instructions night and day, but the old gentleman could never hear them too often because they brought back memories of intense pleasure.

The huntsman's scarlet coat once used to be called 'pink' and anyone who called it red was considered to be an ignorant oaf. The hunting community were never colour-blind as the uninformed have sometimes supposed. The expression 'to be in the pink' derives from the name of a London tailor called

Mr Pink. All fashionable huntsmen once liked to have their expensive coats cut by him because they had enormous respect for his skills.

It was seen as boorish to describe a huntsman's coat as scarlet because it insinuated that he could not afford to be 'in the pink' as he was meant to be. The term was a tactful one. It gave every huntsman the benefit of the doubt.

Now that Mr Pink's tailoring establishment no longer exists, this little snobbery has changed again just when so many had learnt not to commit an embarrassing social error. At this moment it is correct to say that a huntsman hunts, *never, never*, in red, but only 'in a red coat'.

The code-like expressions of the hunt have entered the language and become everyday clichés. Anyone with any 'staying power' who manages to get off to a 'flying start' and feels 'in the pink' as they 'toe the line', while 'never putting a foot wrong' as they 'have a good day', is unwittingly stealing the language and the images of the fox-hunter.

Americans have appropriated 'Have a good day.' In translation the greeting becomes 'Have a nice day.' In the United States this expression is now used to excess. But the American gasoline attendant who repeats it after filling up the car, the chorus of chirpy secretaries in the sky-scraper offices who give this automatic greeting, no longer use it in its original context. When the huntsman 'has a good day', he finds a fox early, he is given a long run, he doesn't break his neck or his horse's legs, and he keeps up with the hounds and is there on the spot when the fox is killed.

Anyone who is 'prominent in his field', and keeps his girlfriend 'on a loose rein' and tries 'to keep her pecker up' for fear she might give him 'the brush off' and ultimately 'ditch' him, is also borrowing the words of the hunt. (A horse pecks when it lands on its knees after a jump and its nose 'pecks' the ground.)

Terms like 'to go to ground', 'to take cover', 'to be flying high', 'to feel ploughed under', 'to draw someone out', or 'draw the line', 'break fresh ground', 'brook no delay' have the same sporting source.

The expression 'a fast woman' also comes from the hunt, and originates from the period when it was considered shocking and louche for a woman to ride astride, as we shall see in the next chapter.

# 10

# The Golden Age

*'If hunting were based on exclusiveness it would have perished long ago.'*
William Bromley-Davenport

In the eighteenth century almost every pack of hounds had its 'hunting parson'. These colourful and sporting ecclesiasts frequently hunted as often as six days a week. They only rested on Sundays, the day when they delivered their sermons. They used to post up announcements informing their parishioners of the time and place of forthcoming meets on the notice-boards of their churches. In the nineteenth century the hunting parson slowly vanished from the field, partly due to a wave of Victorian evangelism.

The public suddenly disapproved of the whole concept of the hunting man of God. 'There is a strong feeling against a clergyman that hunts,' wrote Anthony Trollope in 1868, deploring their decline. 'Their number and wholesome influence on the hunting field is rapidly diminishing.'

The diminution of the 'wholesome influence' of the hunting parson was not only due to religious disapproval. Economic factors added to his decline. The Victorian era has always been called the 'golden age' of the fox-hunt. The sport of kings, which had originally made those who hunted feel 'ennobled' because the monarch permitted only nobles to hunt, suddenly changed its snobberies and its forms. (Horse racing acquired the same name once it was encouraged by the monarchy.)

The Tudors and Stuarts had all been rabid hunters. George

III hunted regularly with the Royal Buckhounds until the day he shook hands with the branch of an oak, mistaking it for the Dutch Ambassador; after that his courtiers felt it was unwise to allow him to follow the hounds. George IV was the first King to prefer to chase the fox rather than the 'carted' tame stags which his predecessors had hunted after wild deer had become virtually extinct. The 'carted' stag was brought to the meet in a wagon, released for the chase and eventually saved by the huntsman from the hounds so that it could live to give more sport.

When George IV declared the fox to be his favourite prey, fox-hunting was seen as an 'ennobling' activity and the fox acquired sudden status. He was regarded as being 'ennobled' by the nobility of those who hounded him.

'Never had the fox the honour of being chased to death by so accomplished a huntsman,' a contemporary wrote of Peter Beckford, one of the best regarded nineteenth-century Masters of Fox-hounds. Peter Beckford was reputed to be so cultured that he could 'bag a fox in Greek, chase a hare in Latin, and clean his stables in Italian'. The concept of the fox being honoured by the courage and culture of those who pursue him is a popular one in nineteenth-century hunting literature.

Although hunting had always been patronised by royalty, curiously it was in the reign of Queen Victoria, a monarch who neither hunted nor approved of the sport, that fox-hunting had its 'golden age'. This mythical golden era was introduced by factors that had little to do with the English throne.

In the nineteenth century, ever-increasing urban industrial expansion created an agricultural collapse that was catastrophic for the farm labourer, but 'magic' for the Quorn. More than half the land that had once grown wheat and other crops was put back to grass. This provided ideal conditions for the fox-hunters because it permitted superb and uninterrupted 'runs'.

The wage of the farm labourer dropped to three shillings per week. William Cobbett described the English peasantry as 'troops of half-starved creatures flocking from the fields'. These 'half-starved creatures' shut the gates after the fox-hunters had galloped by and also mended the broken fences.

The invention of the steam engine was another important factor that helped to bring in a 'golden era' for the fox-hunt. When it was first invented the fox-hunting community saw it as the invention of the Devil. It went chuffing through the countryside belching smoke, breaking the scent of the fox and threatening the lives of the hounds.

A fox-hunting Member of Parliament, Walter Bromley-Davenport, wrote a valedictory poem that describes his horror of the railroad:

*And I looked into its pages*
*And I read the Book of Fate*
*And saw fox-hunting abolished by the State.*
*Saw the airy navvies earthwards*
*Bear the planetary swell*
*And the long projected railroad*
*Made from Halifax to Hell!*

Bromley-Davenport viewed the steam engine with much the same terror and revulsion with which many people today view the nuclear bomb. It would bring an end to the universe as he knew it.

His fears were groundless. The steam engine turned out to be a blessing for the fox-hunt. It brought it new blood. A new type of fox-hunter was brought to life by the railroad, the city-dwelling fox-hunter. Rich city magnates, Members of Parliament, London industrialists, even owners of the dreaded railroads, all started to hunt.

The steam engine enabled them to attend meets that were held far away in the countryside. Special trains were laid on for the new sportsmen. The 'Hunting Specials' carried only cargoes of fox-hunting urbanites wearing their full hunting regalia.

Initially the ancient, traditional, aristocratic fox-hunters were not overjoyed when the 'foreigners' joined 'the field'. But the new city-dwelling hunters brought great wealth to the sport. They paid their subscriptions or 'caps', which helped to pay the hunt servants and feed the hounds. They bought up vast tracts of land for the express purpose of hunting over it. They made the activity so expensive that the small squire and the hunting parson could not compete with the huge equestrian ménàges that they set up. The 'foreigners' bought country houses not because they wanted to live in them but for their weekend hunting. Their stables teemed with stable-boys and grooms.

In the nineteenth century the beautiful Empress of Austria arrived in England with the sole purpose of hunting with the Pytchley. She had heard of the fabulous grass gallops provided by this fashionable pack of hounds and, knowing that her own country could not provide comparable hunting conditions, decided to travel to seek the ideal conditions that she craved.

An ancestor of the Princess of Wales, the 5th Earl of Spencer, was at that time the master of the Pytchley. He had maintained his pack of hounds at considerable personal cost. During the agricultural depression he had been forced to sell his library at Althrop in order to support them. The Earl of Spencer was not only master of the Pytchley, he was also Viceroy of Ireland, and divided his time between ruling Ireland and mastering his hounds in Northamptonshire.

The Earl was a fearless man, who continued to hunt the fox in Ireland in a period of extreme unrest when it was highly dangerous for a hated Englishman in his position to go galloping across the countryside without protection. The British government begged him to desist and pointed out the dangers of assassination – to no avail.

The Earl maintained, 'There is nothing like a good gallop

across the country to drive away dull care.' As the Irish political situation grew more and more incendiary, it brought him more and more cares. As a result, he hunted the more.

Eventually the British government appointed him a special hunting aide-de-camp. Bay Middleton was a huntsman who had also served in the 12th Lancers. He was armed and entrusted with the difficult task of protecting the Earl's life on the hunting field.

In *Elysian Fields*, his book on fox-hunting, Simon Blow describes Bay Middleton as having 'that indefinable charm which the upper classes can be so adept at breeding'. The beautiful Empress of Austria was introduced to him at a Pytchley meet, and there then started a hunting love affair which was to become one of the great Victorian scandals. When the Empress succumbed to Bay Middleton's 'indefinable charm' and brazenly hunted side by side with her lover she made it glamorous for women to hunt. Previously, Victorian society, with its ideal of the gentle white-skinned housebound woman who painted watercolours and had her hair scraped back into a modest centre-parting, had considered it unfeminine for women to hunt. The Empress made female huntresses become supremely fashionable.

She was very much disliked by Queen Victoria because she turned down any royal invitations if they interfered with her pursuit of the fox, and the Queen was not accustomed to such slights. The Empress once paid a visit to Windsor in high summer when the season was over and acceptance of the royal invitation could not cause her distress by preventing her from riding to hounds. After the visit of the Empress, Queen Victoria made a sarcastic little jotting in her diary. 'She spoke with delight of having hunted each day since she arrived!!!'

In the language of the hunt, the Austrian huntress 'broke fresh ground'. Lonely and over-chaperoned, many Victorian society women whose lives were spent in breeding, or waiting for a marriage that would enable them to breed, took to the chase. Fox-hunting provided everything that was lacking in lives that were devoted to the dainty and humdrum.

On the hunting field a woman was equal to a man. A woman could be 'in at the kill' just as easily as the hard-riding gentleman with the side-burns and the silk top hat. On the hunting field they heard cursing and foul oaths; only soldiers and prison inmates swear like members of the hunt as they go over their fences. All the cursing and the bad language was music to ears that were meant to be shell-like, ears that had previously only been allowed to hear the genteel tinkle of the piano and the harp.

When Prince Charles goes out hunting, apparently he also enjoys being cursed. In his preface to *The Magic of the Quorn* he writes, 'I remember on one occasion there was a frantic rush to get forward through a gap in a hedge and several people shouted at me in the mêlée.' He described his reaction. 'I'm afraid my response was to maintain a strict calm and to observe that someone had to try and keep up the standard.'

'Prince Charles loves it when they all curse him,' insist the women who hunt alongside him. 'He's not treated like the future King when he's out with the Quorn. It's the only time that he feels human.'

Like Prince Charles, Victorian women, who were over-protected and sick to death of receiving only deference, loved the violence and hurly-burly of the hunt.

They were more at risk than men because they rode side-saddle. Conventional society deemed it unseemly for women to ride astride. The side-saddle gives the rider very little balance. It twists the body at an unnatural angle. The beautiful long black skirts of the Victorian lady draped down the flank of her horse looked immensely graceful. But those lovely skirts hid the dangerous raised pommel of her saddle – the leather hump around which her knee was hooked to prevent her from falling. In an accident, the side-saddle rider often remains hooked to her horse and is not thrown free. If the horse comes down at a fence and rolls on her, she can be impaled by the pommel and crushed to death.

Laura, Duchess of Marlborough, rode side-saddle in the 1930s when there was no longer any social stigma against a woman riding astride. 'I did it just because I loved the look of the clothes,' she told me. 'Breeches have never been flattering for women. I was lucky – I was always very thin, but breeches are disastrous for women with fat bottoms.'

She remembers her leg being broken as she was going through a gate. 'It was broken very slowly and painfully by that idiot Lord Ashcombe.' 'How did he break it?' I asked her. 'I was going through a gate and he tried to come charging through the same gate – he was on my left. His stirrup got entangled with my stirrup. There were masses of horses in front of us and you know how fresh horses hate confusion. Ashcombe's horse suddenly shied and started reversing, and it took my leg with it. My horse was advancing and his horse was reversing. It was a nightmare . . . '

As the Duchess was riding side-saddle she was unable to disentangle her stirrup as she could have done if she'd been riding astride. She was frightened that she would fall backwards and break her spine. She remembers screaming at Lord Ashcombe, 'You are breaking my leg, you idiot!' She then heard her leg crack and she screamed again from the pain, 'Now you have broken my leg, you stupid idiot!'

After her leg had been broken her stirrup somehow was disentangled from Lord Ashcombe's stirrup. Lacking gallantry, he galloped away with the rest of the riders leaving her in agony. 'It was ghastly finding myself riding a horse side-saddle with a fractured leg – you see, I couldn't dismount.' She was fortunate to be saved by a groom who recognised she was in extreme distress. She was taken off to the local hospital. 'Cottage Hospital used to be the most dreadful place. We all seemed to end up there. Cottage Hospital was near Craven Lodge. After I got out of there I always had it written in my hunting boots, "I don't want to be taken to Cottage Hospital, Craven Lodge."'

Once the Duchess was admitted to hospital she was examined by a nurse, who shook her head gravely and said that she feared they would have to cut her hunting boot.

'It was maddening,' the Duchess said. 'My leg was throbbing and swelling up by the minute, and the idiotic nurse seemed to think I would prefer to have my leg amputated rather than ruin my boot. Of course it was an expensive boot. Looking back – it was a really beautiful boot. But that was hardly the point . . .'

In the hospital the Duchess's leg was put in traction. There were two other victims of hunting accidents in the hospital, and they kept sneaking into her room. 'I had the most awful time with those two men,' she said. 'They were in a much more advanced stage of recovery than I was. One of them was that dreadful David Beatty. He was spinning around in a wheelchair and the other creature, whose name I can't remember, could hobble about on crutches. And both of them took advantage of my horrible situation. They took it in turns to molest me, seeing that I was totally incapacitated. Both of them behaved abominably.'

It was a surrealistic post-hunting scene that the Duchess described, the injured huntsmen hunting the bedridden huntress. 'Hunting used to be freedom,' the Duchess said to me. 'I used to adore it. Now when I look back I don't think we knew what we were doing. Even when I was young I never could bear it when they dug the fox out. I always cantered away and avoided that part. I could never watch all the blood and the horror. And now that I'm old I've become so fond of animals . . . I really don't know what to say about hunting . . . I think that when we were young – we just didn't think . . . '

Hunting in the 1930s, the Duchess of Marlborough could choose her saddle, and she accepted the responsibility if her love of the costume that went with it brought her unnecessary pain and unpleasantness.

The Victorian pioneer huntswomen were condemned to be perched vulnerably on the dangerous saddles that were meant to give them propriety. They were determined to give birth to daughters who were 'fast women', but they themselves were still imprisoned by the convention that no 'lady' must ride astride.

However, seeing the hunting field as a gate to freedom from the claustrophobic confines of their domestic social role, they accepted the limitations of the skew-whiff saddles they were allotted. They took the risks and were frequently 'pommelled' – a very nasty term describing a horrific accident that involves being impaled through the stomach with the raised part of the saddle.

Women who had been languishing in depression exacerbated by the monotony and tedium of their lives left the plushy comfort of their homes, abandoned their embroidery and rode off to the meet, where they drank champagne from stirrup cups, and where some over-chaperoned spinsters mixed with men for the first time. They found that they looked much better mounted than they looked on the ground. A short, squat woman could take on the beauty and the stature of her thoroughbred horse. Surtees, the great novelist of the fox-hunt, wrote, 'Women never look so well as when one comes in wet and dirtied from hunting.'

Rejoicing in a new-found sexual power in which they could attract the opposite sex even when their faces were bleeding from bramble scratches and splattered with mud, many Victorian women used the fox-hunt as if it were a marriage market. They galloped alongside the bewhiskered men casting seductive glances from under their provocative hunting veils. Daughters of newly-rich industrialists seized the opportunity to meet the aristocracy on the hunting field. Love affairs started. The girls with the silk top hats and sexy veils found that the chase gave them a chance to make good matches.

The fox-hunt gave the Victorian woman more scope for

social climbing than it provided her father or brother with. It is the claim of the fox-hunter that everyone is equal on the hunting field. This was only partly true in Victorian England. The small farmer on his nag and the impoverished hunting parson were seen as equal to the wealthy aristocrat as they jumped the fences. They often landed in the 'same ditch', though this did not mean they were automatically invited to the hunt dinners and hunt balls. Whereas, if their daughter rode with panache and cut a handsome figure on the field, she could attract the attention of some hunting gentleman and would then find it easy to slither through the social barriers.

Kept women and prostitutes started to appear on the field, their costumes and horses paid for by some hunting lover. This was not considered correct, but as long as they observed the hallowed rules of the hunt and didn't disgrace themselves by cantering through a field of young corn their presence was tolerated. It was seen as bad form if they hunted on the same days that the wives of their lovers were hunting and they were expected to check whether the wives would be turning up at the meet by consulting the grapevine and the network of stable-lads and grooms.

In the First World War women made another break-through. With so many men away fighting in the trenches they took over the hounds and became brilliant masters.

The numbers of women masters have increased steadily through the years. In 1978 there were sixty-nine female Masters of Fox-hounds. By 1982 there were seventy-seven. The galloping emancipation of women has created casualties. Some of their children have suffered as a consequence. If a woman spends most of her days on the hunting field, if she spends the time when she is not hunting either preparing to go hunting, or recovering from a hard day's hunting, her children are unlikely to receive much maternal care.

In the 1920s a new type of hunting figure emerged, the hunting nursing mother. The woman who could deliver her baby, and be back in the saddle riding over the fences in the shortest possible time, was the woman who was the most admired by her group. This fashion for pulling on the hunting boots and the riding breeches the moment the umbilical cord had been severed was not always beneficial to the Baby Buntings who were left behind in the delivery room when 'mother had gone a-hunting'.

In Northamptonshire recently I took a taxi from a local station. My driver was a young woman in her thirties, and as we drove along she suddenly told me that she was feeling desperately depressed. I said I was sorry and asked her what she was depressed by. She told me she was pregnant, and I assumed that she was having an unwanted baby who was probably illegitimate. But her problem was not the one I had imagined. She told me that she was dying to go cub-hunting and she couldn't decide whether she dared to do it. 'But surely you are not going to go cub-hunting when you are pregnant,' I said. I'd rarely heard of a more dangerous ambition. I had a hallucinatory vision of the head of her unborn infant metaphorically cracking up and down on the saddle. I imagined her lying with her pregnant stomach trapped under some massive struggling horse. I saw her kicked in the belly by a passing chestnut mare.

As I feebly murmured about these possible hazards she became stubborn. I realised that by fussing about the risks I'd removed her indecision. She'd become resolute. She would now definitely go cub-hunting and that was that. She said she'd hunted all through her last pregnancy and she was certain she'd get away with it again. As her last cub-hunting pregnancy had progressed so smoothly, it seemed strange that she'd had even a momentary qualm about hunting when carrying her second baby. She never gave me any reasons for her trepidations. She was the first pregnant hunter of fox-cubs that I'd ever encountered. In her role of mother-to-be you might have expected her to have some maternal identification with the mother vixen whose young she was planning to tear apart, but she had none. She was going to track down those little fox-cubs and if she endangered her own child in her pursuit of their blood – that was just too bad. I found her attitudes chilling and felt that they boded ill for the future happiness of her infant.

But if she'd allowed her pregnancy to deprive her of months of hunting, her fierce resentment against the baby who had been the instrument of this deprivation might have proved just as damaging to its emotional well-being in the long run.

# 11
# The Hunt's Children

*'The female of the species.'*

Kipling

I spoke to a Jungian psychotherapist who is the daughter of an Irish female Master of Fox-hounds. 'Mummy mastered the Galway Blazers. She always saw me as so much lower than a hound. It was really awful . . .' she told me.

A daughter of a Welsh Master of Fox-hounds gave this description of her childhood. 'Mummy bought me ten ponies and lots of dogs and she gave me nothing else – but really nothing – I'm sure that's why I'm so odd.'

She remembered, as a child of six, being in great pain from an abscess on her tooth. 'Mummy was very bored and irritated by my abscess because she wanted to go to the blacksmith to get her mare shod. There was some important meet the following day. "Please don't make such a fuss, darling," she said. "We'll attend to your tooth later." She made me get on my pony and we hacked for miles to the blacksmith. I was in agony, my tooth was throbbing like hell. The ride was awful. After the blacksmith had shod Mummy's mare she said, "Now that we are here, darling, why don't we let the blacksmith attend to your tooth? It will save so much time and so much fuss and bother with dentists." So the blacksmith got out all sorts of funny, dirty-looking implements. Mummy kept insisting that he'd had dental training. Anyway he attended to my tooth, and I don't know what the man did to it but it was a horrible experience. And to this day I have trouble with that tooth and London dentists are mystified when they see what's been done to it. I think that the blacksmith must have treated it as if it was a hoof . . . '

The painter, Francis Bacon, also came from an Anglo-Irish sporting background. 'My grandmother hunted. She hunted and she gave parties – that's really all my grandmother did. My mother hunted, she didn't hunt quite as much as my grandmother – but *she hunted.* My father was a horse-trainer – a *failed* horse-trainer.' He emphasised the word 'failed' in order to make the world in which he'd grown up sound as repulsive as possible.

I asked Bacon if he'd ever hunted himself. 'Of course they forced me to hunt. I really *loathed* it. I couldn't bear the whole thing. I found it all ghastly. But those hunting people are so cruel to their children. They are ruthless about making them hunt. And I suspect that the Anglo-Irish may be even more ruthless than the English in that respect.'

In the end Francis Bacon got out of hunting because he developed an allergy to horses and hounds, and started to have the most terrible asthma attacks on the hunting field. 'Even my parents couldn't make me go on. But it was all so horrible I don't really want to talk about it.'

Bacon never goes back to Ireland. He develops an asthma attack if he boards an Irish plane. He can fly to Paris or New York but he becomes ill if he flies to Dublin. I soon stopped questioning him about his dreaded hunting childhood because I noticed that the subject was upsetting him and making him develop a distinct asthmatic wheeze. It is interesting to speculate that lurking somewhere behind the powerful agonised images in his paintings lies the child's horror of the brutality of the hunt and the whole mystique of 'Tally Ho'.

The Irish novelist, Molly Keane (who used to write under the pseudonym M. J. Farrell), also suffered from being the child of a hunting-mad mother. 'You couldn't believe how my mother neglected her children,' she told me. Molly Keane's mother expected her to hunt but never bothered to teach her to ride. She felt that any child that she'd given birth to must know how to hunt automatically, and saw the ability to ride to hounds as hereditary – a skill that could be passed down like a gene in the blood.

In her brilliant novel *The Rising Tide*, Molly Keane has written about the cruelty that a hunting mother inflicts on her two terrified children. Cynthia, Keane's half-monster, half-heroine, has the 'semi-fanatic must hunt attitude which is often stronger in women than in men . . . It was a flame that was part of herself.' When Cynthia hears that Desmond, her adored husband, has been killed in the First World War, she gets on her horse and goes out hunting to the horror both of her dead husband's mother and of the other riders at the meet.

'It is difficult', Molly Keane writes, 'for people who don't bother about hunting to make any sense of Cynthia's strong desire and insistence on hunting this day and causing such unnecessary distress and embarrassment. There are people, and Cynthia was one of them, to whom the mental and physical excitement of hunting are both a religion and a drug . . . The brain is tremendously independent of the body in the excitement of hunting, and that excitement fulfilled, the body is curiously independent of the brain. One is filled with either excitement, fear or content; never, as it were, in slack water.'

Cynthia changes the date of her husband's memorial service so that it doesn't clash with her hunting. This torments her mother-in-law, who sees the change as an unforgivable insult to her son's memory.

Cynthia's two little children, Simon and Susan, are terrified of hunting, but dare not admit their fear even to each other. Their mother has made them regard fear as a deeply shameful emotion. They often vomit before setting off for the meet. They know their mother will be livid if they don't 'go well'. She will be furious if they avoid jumps and cheat by using gates, if they run over a hound, or let their ponies bolt. It will also enrage her if they forget the names of any of the hounds. Most of all they fear her anger if they are the last to be in at the kill.

The more falls they have the better their mother is pleased because she believes that falls will teach them that falling doesn't hurt. When Simon's pony lands on another rider and knocks the man unconscious, Cynthia is not at all disturbed. She sees the accident as happy proof that her son was 'going quite well'.

Molly Keane describes the experience of these terrified children as they follow the hounds. 'Susan and Simon were often borne along for miles with tears pouring down their faces, and everyone said how much they were enjoying themselves and how well they went for children of their age.'

Sometimes Simon and Susan don't have a fall, but they still suffer the mental agony of thinking they are going to. They loathe it when their mother comes up and beats the rumps of their ponies with a stick so that they are forced to ride over huge walls and ditches.

'Their mother also suffered in her way. Cynthia minded dreadfully that they should be such pale, uncourageous children, these children of hers and Desmond's . . . She did not love her children, but she was determined not to be ashamed of them. You had to feel ashamed and embarrassed if your children did not take kindly to blood sports, so they must be forced into them. It was right. It was only fair to them.' Yet, having described so movingly the pain these children suffered on the hunting field, Molly Keane uses the ultimate irony to shock her readers: children who originally loathed the hunt can become brainwashed and grow to love it.

The short-story writer James Stern, in one of his best stories, 'The Broken Leg', has also written a brilliant and chilling description of children at the mercy of the obsessional huntswoman.

Hilda Archer, Stern's fictional mother, 'was known as the

bravest and most intrepid rider throughout the Shires'. She was a woman of 'rigid principles and of two outstanding passions shared by her husband, she loathed physical cowardice and adored fox-hunting'.

She had two young sons, Max and Eliot, but she didn't really know them. They lived in her house and they had a governess. They were very well fed, but she only felt there was any point in getting to know them after she had suffered a devastating accident which blighted her whole life. She had a fall in which she splintered her knee bone so badly that it was found sticking out through her breeches, and she was traumatised by the knowledge she could never hunt again.

Stern then tells the terrifying story of a crippled woman who, knowing she has lost the only thing on earth which has ever given her pleasure, realises that she must get to know her sons. They have suddenly become of use to her. She decides that they have to become expert huntsmen so that she can hunt vicariously through them.

There follows a memorable description of the misery to which this hunting-deprived mother subjects Max, the elder of her sons, when she finds out that he is temperamentally incapable of carrying out her fantasy. She sees him make a fool of himself when his pony runs away with him, and she sees him cry when he is thrown. She realises to her horror that one of her sons is a coward!

> Crawling to his feet, covering his face with his hands, Max moved off the field. As he went he shivered with the cold of weakness, the horror of utter shame. He felt that nothing he did in the future could ever atone for the humiliating performance his mother, father and brother had just witnessed. He knew, moreover, that he had committed a great sin, two sins: he had shown fear while on a horse, and he had 'cried before he was hurt'. In the great hollow abyss of misery that only a child can know, he felt utterly, terribly alone; the whole of his tiny world

> was against him; there was none to whom he could turn; he was doomed. As he went up to his room the word rang out in his head as each foot mounted a stair – Doomed! Doomed! Doomed!

Just as Molly Keane's fearless character, Cynthia, suffers dreadfully when she realises she has produced 'pale uncourageous children', Stern's crippled Hilda Archer suffers acutely when she discovers that she has produced a son who is a coward.

> In the early hours Mrs Archer woke perspiring from a nightmare. Sitting up, she tried to retrieve in her conscious mind what had happened in her sleep; but all she could remember was being surrounded by hunting people in her drawing-room, and whilst she stood alone amongst them they raised their hands and pointed at her. 'Max is a coward!' they murmured in chorus, 'Max is a coward!' Then, breathless and sweating, she had woken. She remained awake till after dawn.

The fictional children of Molly Keane and James Stern suffer not only from fear but from a terror that they may display the symptoms of fear. They also suffer from guilt, for they know that their lack of courage is a source of great pain to their mothers.

But not all children have been made miserable by the parental demand that they must hunt. The real-life children of the Dukes of Somerset were not allowed to hunt more than three days a week until they were five years old. If they hunted six days a week it was feared that it would spoil them.

# 12

# Professor Eysenck's Poll

*'They must have costly clothes,*
*They must have dainty fare,*
*They must have fowls,*
*They must have beasts,*
*To bait, to hunt, to kill.'*

George Turberville

In 1971 Professor Hans Eysenck conducted a curious poll in which he made a statistical survey of the attitudes of Masters of Fox-hounds and then compared them to the attitudes of the average British non-hunting citizen. Perhaps the most interesting facet of his survey was his own attitude towards Masters of Fox-hounds. It is curious that he considered the views of this minority group to be of sufficient importance to be worthy of a detailed and time-consuming study.

According to Professor Eysenck's poll, Masters of Fox-hounds yearn for the reintroduction of the death penalty more than the average citizen. They are also much keener to have flogging reintroduced in British prisons. Whereas the average man in the street had doubts about the slogan 'My Country Right or Wrong', not one single MFH expressed any doubts at all. The test questions put to the masters by the Professor were a little woolly and fatuous, as the questions in many such statistical surveys tend to be. 'A white lie is often a good thing,' was one of the challenging statements with which Eysenck confronted them. They were allowed to answer, 'I strongly agree', 'I agree', 'Don't know or no opinion', 'Disagree', 'Strongly disagree'.

The Masters of Fox-hounds strongly agreed that a white lie was often an excellent thing, which unfortunately proved very little, because in 1971 the average British citizen strongly agreed with this as well.

The stance that the masters took on this important issue still has its interest though, for it conjures up an astonishing image of scarlet-coated figures in velvet jockey caps white-lying their heads off on the hunting field. And what would be the nature of the humanitarian untruthfulness of the masters? If they allowed their hounds to devour some poor old lady's favourite cat and saw to it that all evidence of its bloody demise was destroyed, would they think they were telling a white lie if they said that they had never seen her pet? She certainly wouldn't be happy to be informed that her darling Tabby had met with such a truly horrible death. It might well be much kinder to shield her. The border between black and white lies has always been hard to define.

'An occupation by a foreign power is better than war' was another of the bombshell tests to which Eysenck subjected the masters. And on this issue they all exploded with a violence that was far greater than that of the average man. Until I read this esoteric survey I had never really considered how calamitous the invasion of a foreign power would be for fox-hunting. Naturally, the masters would scream for war at any price. Their reaction made perfect sense.

From the evidence presented in Professor Eysenck's questionnaire, Masters of Fox-hounds can be inconsistent in their attitudes. They believed that 'The Church should attempt to increase its influence on the life of the nation.' They also believed that 'People should realise that their greatest obligation was to their family.' It was in their attitude towards extra-marital sex that they became perverse and displayed a liberalism far greater than that of the average man. None of them felt that adultery was wrong.

'The hunting fraternity are notoriously lascivious and in the season the night air of Melton Mowbray is loud with the sighs of adulterers,' wrote Paul Johnson. Maybe he found the confidence to write this libellous statement after studying the findings of Professor Eysenck's poll.

The hunt provides unique and comfortable facilities which encourage adultery. Once the hounds set off, the riders leave their empty horse-boxes parked in fields and lanes and woods all over the countryside. There is hay in the horse-box and there are horse-rugs. In the turmoil and confusion of the chase it is impossible for husbands and wives to know the whereabouts of their marriage partners – they could be anywhere. They could be riding ten miles away – they could be in hospital. An adulterous couple can slip away to make love in the warm and sexy hay-scented privacy of an abandoned horse-box and enjoy all the anonymity that is provided by the drive-in motel. There are so many horse-boxes at every hunt that it would be a truly daunting task for the most jealous spouse to search them all.

Love-making inside a closed horse-box parked in the no man's land of some remote and muddy field gives the lovers the feeling they have discovered a desert-island paradise where the rules of the world no longer apply. It may be for that reason that the Masters of Fox-hounds saw no clash between their support of adultery and their fervent belief in the unity of the family.

When the Professor studied the racial attitudes of the Masters of Fox-hounds, it emerged that they felt that 'Jews were as valuable citizens as any other group'.

Presumably they were estimating the worth of the Jews solely in relation to their value to the hunt. Since the Victorian 'golden age' of the fox-hunt many Jewish industrialists have taken up hunting as a means of assimilation into British society, and they have bought up land which the hunt has hunted over in peace without being hassled by the dreaded farmer, often the plague of the sport. Their value was rightly recognised by the masters.

Although the huntsmen under examination displayed no anti-Semitism, their racial tolerance did not extend to coloured people. They all believed that it was best to keep such people 'in their own districts and schools in order to prevent too much contact with whites'. They also saw coloured people as 'innately inferior to white people'. In the history of fox-hunting coloured people have not been very 'prominent on the field', and the masters viewed them with little respect. Another salient point that emerged from this peculiar statistical poll was the unusual attitude of the Masters of Fox-hounds towards suicide. They never thought about it. They had no opinion about it. They did not care whether self-inflicted death was morally right or wrong – an indifference which was not at all typical of the views of the other citizens with whom they were compared. It set them in a special category. Perhaps their chosen calling, in which every fence and ditch could be seen as an invitation to suicide, had forced them to build up a defensive indifference to self-inflicted death.

Their attitudes also veered away from the norm in their approach to birth control and abortion. They were against any government or Church interference in these matters, seeing it as an invasion of the privacy of the individual. They felt very strongly that privacy should be respected because they felt paranoid at the way their own privacy was being continually invaded by those who are trying to deprive them of their right to hunt.

On finishing Professor Eysenck's study I wondered how long it had taken him to complete it. I assumed that most of his work had been done in the summer before the hunting season began. It seemed unlikely that the pollsters had followed those hard-riding masters over the timbers, shouting questions against the wind as they tried to establish whether these wealthy huntsmen considered capitalism immoral.

And when the exhausted masters returned from a hard

day's hunting, it was to be hoped that the pollsters had allowed them to pull the boots off their frozen feet before they started to pester them with unanswerable posers. 'Does the so-called underdog deserve little sympathy or help from successful people?'

I found myself wondering who on earth this painstaking poll had been compiled for. It was difficult to imagine the individual who would feel that his understanding of life had been enhanced by its findings. Even the masters themselves would not be all that interested in their own attitudes. Why would they want to read about their attitudes when they already knew them?

But then on further reflection I decided I was being unfair to Professor Eysenck. He had done a very thorough job on an original subject. I was glad to be informed that all Masters of Fox-hounds were incorrigible white liars. For that startling fact alone I felt that the Professor's laborious study had been very worthwhile.

# 13
# The Car-Hunter

*'Life would be very pleasant if it were not for its enjoyments.'*
Surtees

The mad-keen car-hunter is almost more threatening to the modern hunt than is the saboteur. Having taken up 'the occupation of the élite', car-hunters can behave with an arrogance that surpasses that of most riders, and they make the sport unpopular.

Throughout history the mounted human has always felt a natural superiority to the human being who is on foot. The modern British huntswoman wearing her hair-net and her 'bowler' trots past the man in the lane, and when her mare splatters him with mud and water it doesn't always occur to her that any apology is necessary. She may not bother to turn round to see what she has done to him. She is out hunting. She trots on. She is so engrossed in her occupation that she barely casts a cold eye.

The hunt often behaves as if it has sole control of the British roads, making little attempt to keep their horses in to the side. 'I was on my bicycle,' a woman from Northampton told me. 'I was trying to get to work and I got behind this bloody hunt. They were going to their meet and they were going at a very leisurely pace. The whole road was blocked solid with hounds and horses. Can you beat it – they kept me behind for five miles! Would they make way to let me pass – you must be joking! Finally I lost my temper and I gave a scream. They were making me late for work and I don't approve of hunting. I screamed so loudly that I made some of their horses shy. Then they turned round. "What's the matter with you?" they asked me.

'"I want you to make way so that I can get to work," I told them.

'"We didn't know that you wanted to get past," they said. They were as rude as anything.

'"What the hell did you think I wanted?" I asked them. I was in a boiling temper.

'"We thought you were a hunt follower," some stupid character in a red coat said to me.

'It made me so angry that I could have happily killed the lot of them. How dare they assume that I was a hunt follower? Especially as I'm one of the people who would vote to get hunting abolished.'

The keen car-hunter who follows the hunt ceases to see himself as a motorist. He will say that he is going hunting just as if he were a rider. While he is on the roads as a person who is out hunting, he can become uncharacteristically reckless and selfish in the management of his vehicle and he acquires all the hunter's scorn for the non-hunter.

Car-hunters are dreaded by the hunt because the horses find it difficult to get past the snarling traffic congestion they create in the lanes. The car-hunters often leave their cars parked wherever they feel inclined and they are stubborn in their refusal to move them. They are also the bane of those whose profession requires the free use of British roads. I spoke to a Leicestershire plumber who supported the hunt in the sense that he liked their British tradition. He would now vote to have hunting abolished because their car-followers are making his life untenable.

'I get an emergency call,' he said. 'Someone's pipe has burst and there's water pouring through their house. Will those hunt followers move their cars to let me through . . . No way . . . Some of them are real bastards. They don't think that anyone has got anything better to do than hunt. Sometimes I've had my hand on my horn and they knew I was frantic and they ignored me. They just went on gazing through their binoculars. You couldn't believe it!'

The plumber said he'd seen car-hunters refuse to move for the police. 'You get a police car with its blue light flashing and its siren going and the hunt followers won't let it past. They simply ignore it. They don't care if some poor girl has just been raped. They go on sitting in their cars looking for a fox through their binoculars . . . '

Having listened to descriptions of car-hunters, I decided I would have to car-hunt myself. I went to a meet that was being held by the Pytchley on the site of the Battle of Naseby. Although I had been warned that hordes of car-followers now attend every hunt, I was still astonished by their numbers. There seemed to be at least five hundred car-loads of car-hunters as opposed to about eighty riders.

Long before the hounds arrived at the meet the car-hunters had created chaos in the lanes of the surrounding countryside. Cars were creeping along bumper to bumper. A rural peaceful setting had suddenly acquired all the aggravating conditions of a major city in peak rush-hour.

The riders turning up at the meet sported their beautiful costumes as if they wore a military uniform. The car-hunters who turned up wore less spectacular attire, but they too had hunting clothes which they flaunted like a uniform. The tweed cap for the man, the tweed skirt and tweed beret for the woman seemed to be *de rigueur*. The clothes of the riders were flamboyant and colourful, in startling contrast to a bleak and wintry British landscape, whereas the uniform of the car-hunters laid a respectful emphasis on the autumnal hue. In their dull browns, their olives and their greens they made no contrast at all. In their bulky quilted jackets and inevitable green rubber wellingtons the car-hunters were like chameleons, they merged with the cold countryside.

# THE CAR-HUNTER

The hounds arrived late for the meet that day. Their scarlet-coated huntsman had enormous difficulty herding them unscathed through the traffic. When they finally arrived the car-hunters abandoned their vehicles and rushed into the field from which the hunt was due to start.

When I joined them I was instantly approached by a fierce-looking woman wearing traditional car-hunter's uniform. 'I hope you are not an anti,' she said. Her tone was menacing. 'I'm just here to watch the hunt,' I explained. She was a powerful-looking woman with iron-grey curls and a forceful, booming voice. She looked very fit from all her car-hunting. I felt that it would be a courageous anti who would have the nerve to challenge her. She was carrying a shooting stick and gripped it like a weapon. She had such confidence, and such command, that she gave one the feeling she could easily summon her fellow car-hunters and turn them into a pack which would fall on any isolated hunt saboteur and tear him limb from limb.

'We get the anti's here,' she said. 'We expected them today, but they haven't turned up yet. Maybe they couldn't find out where the meet was being held. Lately we try to be discreet. When we advertise the meets we only do it very discreetly.'

She said that she was sorry that no anti's had turned up. She would have liked me to see them. 'They arrive in vans,' she said. 'You couldn't believe how horrible they look. They are so sordid. The anti's are the only sordid thing about hunting . . . '

She was a retired customs officer, and said that she car-hunted six days a week. Feeling bemused, I wondered what had led her to become this fanatical huntswoman. Maybe as a customs officer this energetic character had been hunting all her life. She had once hunted in the suitcases of weary airline passengers. Now in her retirement she had not really changed her occupation, she had merely changed her prey. Whereas once she had spent her days in keen pursuit of drugs and other contraband, she had now discovered a livelier quarry, devoting all her zeal and passions to chasing the fox.

The general mood at the Pytchley meet was very festive that day. After weeks of frost which had made all hunting impossible, both riders and car-hunters had the exhilaration of those who have escaped from the frustrations of any emotional deprivation. The foot-followers handed round free stirrup-cups of sherry in the old tradition which the hunt itself has now mostly abandoned. The riders looked with aristocratic scorn and obvious annoyance at the glasses of sherry that the foot-followers were consuming. The riders were the warriors who were just about to go into glorious battle, but the car-followers had surpassed them in their retention of an ancient hunting tradition.

The vehicle hunters were not about to risk their necks, but they were the ones who were giving themselves Dutch courage. The riders were offered no alcoholic encouragement at all as they valiantly battled to stop their fresh and over-excited horses from kicking or trampling the hordes of over-enthusiastic car-hunters.

Although some of the car-hunters appeared to know the rules of the sport just as well as any equestrian huntsman, some of them didn't. Unemployed youths on motor-bikes would come roaring up to the meet, keen to have a good day's hunting and 'revving up' their engines, unconcerned about the effect the noise of their powerful machines might have on the horses.

I saw an old gentleman wearing a top hat. He had handlebar whiskers and was beautifully dressed in traditional hunting gear. He was riding a mettlesome 'grey'. This remarkable figure and his horse could have stepped out of the pages of a Victorian back number of *Punch*.

It was very soon obvious that this elegant and ancient man was having great trouble trying to control the mettle of his 'grey'. The animal was bucking, it was rearing, it was going crab-wise. The old gentleman was coping admirably, but his face looked grim.

A young woman drew up at the meet in her Land Rover. She got out of her car, brought her children into the field and stationed herself right behind the old fellow's raging animal. 'Look at the bow-wows,' she said to her baby as she pointed at the hounds.

The old gentleman had done everything a correct huntsman can do to issue a danger warning. At the best of times a horse, however quiet, can kick. Horses that are famously vicious, and almost certain to kick, have a red ribbon tied to their tail. The 'grey' was wearing a very large scarlet ribbon.

The young woman seemed to have complete confidence in the horsemanship of the old gentleman. She ignored one of the 'mother's milk' rules of the stables, 'Don't get behind a horse's hooves.' By neglecting this vital rule she became the triumphant exception that proved it. The young woman and her children went unhurt. Standing close behind a rearing, furious and uncontrollable horse she held up her infant son so that, mathematically, he was perfectly positioned to be the victim of the most horrible accident. If the 'grey' had happened to lash out, the keen young car-huntswoman had guaranteed that her baby would receive an iron-clad hoof dead centre in the face. 'Look at the gee gee, William,' she said cheerfully.

The young woman and her family were saved by Providence rather than personal prudence. The huntsman suddenly blew his horn and gathered up the hounds. The whole field moved off taking the bewhiskered top-hatted old gentleman and his evil-tempered horse with them.

The hunt was on. My driver was a novice and had never car-hunted before. Both of us were soon to learn what the joys of car-hunting were all about.

As we left the meet we funnelled into a narrow lane. There were cars to the back of us, cars to the front of us. Only the unemployed youths on motor-bikes who did stunt tricks in and out of the ditches had any 'pace'. They were the only ones who volleyed and thundered.

We remained at a stand-still. As we sat entrapped, the ex-customs officer came walking masterfully past the row of stationary vehicles. She tapped on the windscreens of car after car and she asked their drivers for a 'cap' or a subscription fee. She didn't have the traditional velvet jockey cap that the real hunt passes round when asking for money, but when this stern woman demanded a 'cap' she seemed more greedy than any huntsman could ever be. Wedged in by traffic, no one could escape her. Shamed by her ardent devotion to the sport, the drivers handed her their pounds. With so many stationary cars backed up over such a large area, at the end of the day she must have made quite a 'killing'.

As I looked at the rows of cars that blocked the lane in front of us, I started to develop claustrophobia. Where was the enjoyment in subjecting oneself to the boredom and frustration of sitting trapped for hours in traffic?

I understood why the plumber complained that car-hunters prevented him from making emergency house-calls. If any plumber had tried to get through the section of the countryside commandeered by followers of the Pytchley that day, it would not have been ill-will on the part of the car-hunters if he had failed. They would not have let him through because they would not have been able to let him through.

The traffic problem was not improved by all the horse-boxes which were dotted round the little threading lanes. The riders had ridden off to enjoy the pleasures of the chase and there was an arrogance in the way many of them had left their horse-boxes so blatantly badly parked. No traffic warden was likely to give a huntsman a ticket; no traffic warden could have got to the scene of the parking crime.

We went edging miserably on. Sometimes we came to a crossroads and faced an agonising dilemma. Which lane had the worst congestion? Which way should we turn? Whichever decision we made, it always seemed to be the wrong one.

We were not even spectators to the glories of the hunt. The horses and their riders had galloped away cross-country and by now were probably hunting in another part of England. It felt sad and humiliating to have 'lost the hounds' so quickly. The hedges bordering the lanes were so high we could see only them. The equestrian hunters had all the freedom and the fun and the mobility. They had all the privileges. The car-hunters remained the prisoners of their machines.

Sometimes they got out of their cars and climbed on a gate, or they went to stand in a field where they stood staring through binoculars. But they didn't seem to be able to see anything, it was a damp and freezing winter's day and the prospect of hanging around in a desolate field vainly hoping to catch a glimpse of the hounds was not appealing.

We car-hunted for another joyless hour and the experience didn't improve. 'Shall we give up and go home?' I asked my driver. She was as keen to stop car-hunting as I was. It took us a long time to get home. Extricating ourselves from the chaos created by our fellow car-hunters was not easy. We had not seen one horse do one single jump. We felt frustrated. We felt vaguely to blame.

# 14

# The Magic of the Quorn

*'Come away, my brave sportsmen, away*
*'Tis weather as cheery as May*
*We'll off to the meet*
*Good friendship to greet.'*

Tom Firr (legendary Victorian huntsman of the Quorn)

Although my first day of car-hunting had turned out to be dull and disappointing I still felt that there must be more to the sport than met the eye. Why should so many people adore it with such passion? I wondered if I'd missed the point because I'd tried to car-hunt with a novice rather than a professional.

I was told that in my local village there was a retired widower called Jimmy Herbert who was a passionately keen car-hunter. Apparently he rarely missed a day with the hounds. I approached him and asked if I could accompany him the next time he went out. He was very enthusiastic and agreeable, and said that he was planning to hunt with the Quorn the very next day.

He told me to bring a flask of whisky and some sandwiches. I learned from Jimmy Herbert that serious car-hunters, who call themselves huntsmen as if there was no distinction between themselves and the riders, follow some of the traditional rituals of the chase very strictly. Equestrian huntsmen have always ridden with silver flasks in their pockets or attached to their saddles. A light flask is a practical functional object for any rider. It enables him to take a swig of warming alcohol while galloping 'hell for leather' over the countryside. The silver flask serves no useful function for car-hunters. As they spend so much time sitting stationary in their vehicles they could easily bring a bottle of whisky to the meet and consume it at their leisure from glasses. But they like to swig like libertines from flasks. The gesture gives them a feeling of motion, a sensation which is very hard to achieve in their curiously static sport that is peripheral to another, older sport.

Jimmy Herbert was a friendly little gnome-like man dressed in the obligatory attire of tweeds and green wellingtons. He was clearly very excited by the day's hunting that lay ahead of us. He was 'raring to go'. As we set off he smashed his foot down on the accelerator of his battered little Ford. I was reminded of the way that horses stamp their hooves in their longing to be off.

Jimmy Herbert told me that he hunted at least four days a week. As a pensioner he spent most of his pension on petrol. Till his retirement he had been a worker on the Leicestershire roads. Two years before he had suffered a tragedy. His wife had died of cancer, and he still felt devastated by her loss and grieved for her from morning till night. After a long and happy marriage her death had come as such a shock to him that he knew he was never going to recover from the blow. If it wasn't for hunting he didn't know what he would do.

He had found the summers when the fox-hunting season ceased almost intolerable, he felt so frantic and lonely living on his own. He'd never learnt to cook and he found it very hard to cope with his own housework. He mostly lived on cheese, partly because he wanted to save his money for petrol so that he could hunt as much as he wanted – partly because cheese required no preparation. If you ate chunks of cheese you didn't have to cook and wash up plates.

By Christmas he already began to dread the arrival of summer. In the months when there was no hunting, he never managed to find anything worthwhile to do with his time. His late wife had loved flowers and together they had made a beautiful garden. After she died he'd dug it up and grassed it over. He didn't feel like gardening now that she was no longer there to enjoy the flowers. In the summer he mowed the lawn, but he didn't find that very stimulating. He hated watching television, he found most of the programmes so stupid. He went racing sometimes, but he didn't love it like he loved hunting. Racing was not the same . . .

Jimmy Herbert had a despairing expression on his face while he was telling me about his current situation. Then quite suddenly, as if he felt embarrassed to have burdened a stranger with his personal problems, he changed the subject. He made a deliberate effort to talk about a more cheerful topic.

On the windscreen of his little car there were lots of coloured stickers which bore the names of the many packs of hounds that he'd hunted with in the past. 'Those stickers are asking for trouble!' he said. His whole mood had changed. Once he was talking about anything that was connected with the hunt, he could temporarily forget his grief. He became ebullient and boyish and happy. He told me with gleeful amusement that he had many friends who had sported similar hunt stickers on the front windows of their cars. The stickers had been spotted by members of the anti-blood sports groups. The anti's had reacted with great anger. They had picked up some stones and the offending, stickered windscreens had been smashed to smithereens.

'I like to have my stickers up,' Jimmy Herbert said. 'For me it is worth the risk.'

He told me that your windscreen was always in danger every time you went hunting. If the anti's didn't bash it in, one of the horses was quite likely to kick it in. The other thing at risk was the side-mirror of your car. Passing horses often ripped it off as they tried to get past your vehicle in the narrow lanes.

'Doesn't a horse get hurt if it rips off a side-mirror?' I asked him.

Apparently lots of horses were hurt that way. Jimmy had

seen many a horse with a nasty gash on its flank. When that kind of accident occurred he blamed the riders for bad horsemanship. They shouldn't try to squeeze past the cars of the car-hunters when the gap in the road was too narrow. Some of them became impatient and he saw no excuse for that.

Jimmy Herbert felt that the mounted huntsman ought to adapt his skills so that the immense vehicle presence provided by car-hunters became an obstacle that had to be surmounted with expertise as if it were a postern rail, a double bank, a bull fence or some other hurdle traditionally encountered when people have ridden off in pursuit of the fox.

He seemed to be rather amused by the activities of the hunt saboteurs. He accepted their opposition to his beloved sport without rancour. It was part of the fun, part of the danger. It all added to the sport. He told me that he'd hunted with the Fernie a few weeks previously and a hunt saboteur had turned up and tried to misdirect the hounds. 'He'd learnt to blow the horn so beautifully that he had us all laughing. The fellow who is the current huntsman of the Fernie didn't like the saboteur being so expert. You ought to have seen his face. He didn't hate that sab for trying to put an end to hunting. He knew that anti could easily take his job.'

As we drove to the meet, Jimmy kept tooting on his horn and waving to other drivers on the roads. 'Are you hunting with the Quorn today?' he would shout. The answer always seemed to be 'Yes.'

'I was out with the Cottesmore yesterday,' Jimmy would bellow to his friends through his car window.

'How was your day?' his fellow huntsmen would ask him.

'Good. Very good. I saw three foxes,' he'd answer.

'I wonder if Prince Charles will be hunting today,' he said to me. 'In a way I hope that he won't. Once the rumour gets round that "Charlie boy" is hunting you can't move for the cars. It can really ruin your day. And then all his security men block the lanes and it ruins the sport for all of us.'

'Does Prince Charles go to the meet when he hunts?' I asked him.

'No, he doesn't. He usually joins very quietly once the hounds have found a fox. And sometimes he doesn't start hunting till second horse.'

'Second horse' is the point in the hunt when the master and the huntsmen dismount from their exhausted horses, and the grooms who have been following the hunt's progress in horse-boxes bring them fresh ones on which they finish the day. In Victorian times almost everyone who hunted had a 'second horse', but now it has become an expensive luxury which few can afford.

'We may not get Prince Charles, but I bet we'll get people from all over England hunting today,' Jimmy Herbert said.

I had not realised that car-hunters were prepared to travel very long distances to follow the pack of their choice. Jimmy told me that most of them were very fussy. If they had a local pack of hounds they had no respect for, they refused to hunt with it. They only wanted to follow the best packs – the Quorn, the Belvoir, the Pytchley, the Cottesmore, the Fernie and the Melton Mowbray. They were prepared to drive from the other side of the British Isles to do so.

'The Quorn is the cream of the packs,' Jimmy said. 'You can't beat a day with the Quorn. We ought to get a very good turn-out.'

I dreaded the sound of the big turn-out. It boded badly. It looked as if we were fated to have even worse traffic conditions than I'd experienced hunting with the Pytchley.

And indeed we were. As we approached the spot where the hounds were meeting, the build-up of cars grew worse and worse. We were soon reduced to an agonising creep, eternally edging and stopping and starting. My back was already aching as we made our snail-like and uncomfortable, jerky progress. We were trapped behind a vast and monstrous vehicle with an enormous rotating steel belly that mixed concrete.

'I know the driver of that one,' Jimmy said to me with a wink. 'He's a very keen huntsman.'

'You mean he's hunting!' I was astonished. 'You mean he's hunting in that huge thing!'

Jimmy laughed at my naivety. 'That man is hunting all right. He rarely misses a day. He shouldn't do it – but there you are. I used to do the same myself before I retired. When I was working on the roads I often used to go hunting in vehicles that belonged to the local council. When you get a beautiful day and the hounds are meeting in the neighbourhood – it's very hard to make a huntsman waste his time filling in holes, or putting tarmac on the roads.'

Later in the day Jimmy Herbert pointed out numbers of monstrous and cumbersome vehicles, pantechnicons, articulated lorries, juggernauts and so on. An innocent would have thought they were just travelling through the countryside and going about government or other serious business. This assumption would have been quite incorrect – their drivers had all gone hunting.

As we crept at our dismal pace through the lanes stuck behind the purloined concrete-mixer, I started to hope that the traffic was so bad that we would be late and miss the Quorn meet. I dreaded the idea of a whole day spent circling round the countryside at this horrible, kerb-crawling speed. If we could only arrive at the meet after the hounds had moved off – maybe we could give up the whole idea of hunting and drive quietly home.

All these foolish hopes were soon dashed. Finally, very painfully, we reached the meet on time. I should have realised that Jimmy Herbert was far too experienced a car-hunter to allow us to be late. He had counted on the traffic congestion that we were likely to encounter. By arriving to pick me up so early he'd given us a two-hour leeway.

# 15

# Dressing for the Part

*'The magic in Leicestershire is still there.'*
HRH Prince Charles, Prince of Wales

The Quorn meet was very pleasant after the awful drive that we'd had to get to it. It was a great joy to get out of the car, and very agreeable to be offered a stirrup cup of port.

Jimmy Herbert pointed to the colourful array of horses, hounds and riders, and he looked proud, happy and paternal, as if he had fathered the lot of them.

'Now that's the cream,' he said. 'I've brought you to see the cream. You'll never see better than this.'

We were certainly looking at a beautiful hunting scene. It was frosty and the British sky for a moment was very clear. The horses champed with excitement. They frothed – they reared – they did everything one hoped they'd do. I decided that from my sparse experience of car-hunting I only liked attending the meet. I liked staring childishly at the gleaming horses and examining the costumes of the individual riders. I enjoyed watching the hounds and observing the way that the huntsman recognised every animal in his large pack and kept them in order by calling them by name. To the outsider the hounds looked indistinguishable one from another. The convivial atmosphere of the meet was attractive. Stirrup cups of port seemed intoxicating in the morning.

Years before when I had followed the North Down Harriers in Ulster, the meet had been the only part of the hunting ritual that I'd enjoyed, and now that I was car-hunting the fox, rather than horse-riding after the hare, my reaction was exactly the same.

It struck me that the meets held by the North Down Harriers had been very unstylish events compared with those held by the Leicestershire fox-hunters. The Quorn followers would have been horrified by the attire of the North Down riders with all their wellingtons and their bowlers held on by elastic. Nor would they have been impressed by the breeding of most of the horses – all the broken-down old mares who looked ready to be put out to pasture, and the shaggy ungroomed cobs who seemed to have just stepped out of the shafts of a farm-cart.

Still, I had enjoyed the inactivity of the North Down meets, but my enjoyment was always marred by the knowledge that this safe inactivity was not going to last. The huntsman would soon blow his horn, the hounds would move off and we would be in serious pursuit of the hare. Then there would be all those hellish hours of riding an uncontrollable and insanely over-excited pony over countryside riddled with dangerous ditches and barbed wire.

Car-hunting with Jimmy Herbert, I felt very grateful that the meet I was now enjoying would not be ruined for me by that ancient dread. When the hounds moved off I was not going to be expected to show any valour. All I had to fear was very bad traffic congestion ahead of us. At worst this might be very aggravating, but at least we wouldn't be travelling at 'break-neck speed', and I had to be grateful for that.

The Quorn meet was held on the lawn of a private house with an hospitable owner. The riders were given a stirrup cup, unlike those who had ridden with the Pytchley. This was nicer for the car- and foot-hunters, for they were not made to feel undeservedly privileged.

The theatricality and beauty of the display put on by the hunt seemed its own justification. All the hunting prints that one had seen since childhood made one feel that just such a scene had to exist, the dreary British countryside demanded it. Something had to break the drabness of such a grim winter landscape, with its leafless trees and its cold bleak expanse of lifeless fields.

The English winter days have always seemed unbearably long for those who live in remote rural areas. The months drag by. They bring only unchanging bad weather and frequent bouts of influenza, with little to alleviate the uneventfulness and the boredom of the average countryman's life. The hunt has always provided a valuable cure for the great English malaise of winter melancholia. It has brought drama and danger and spectacle to those forced to spend many months without flowers and sunlight and stimulation. It has provided a necessary festive social focus and an astonishing amount of employment.

'Leicestershire and a lot of English agricultural communities would collapse if the hunt was ever banned,' a local farmer said to me. 'Literally thousands of people would be thrown out of work.'

British corn merchants, hay merchants and fence-menders are amongst those whose professional well-being is most dependent on the patronage of the hunt. A horse which is expected to hunt all winter has to be given hay and it has to be corn-fed, despite the exorbitant cost of these agricultural commodities. Opponents of blood sports resent the fact that so much of the national supply of corn and hay still goes to hunting horses rather than cattle and other livestock.

Critics of fox-hunting also dislike the role of the fence-menders, who follow the progress of the hunt and are employed to repair any ravages that the horses have inflicted on the countryside.

'I think it's disgusting that so many men spend their lives fence-mending,' a vociferous anti said to me. 'Why should they be paid to repair damage that should never have happened in the first place?'

A retired Major who once served with the Brigade of

Guards gave me this response to what he called the 'liberal squeakings of the anti's'. 'I don't know what those stupid wet anti's are thinking of,' he said to me. 'Just think of the things most people have to do to earn their living . . . Do you think that most of the things that provide employment are really valuable? So why do the anti's have to go and attack the poor fence-menders? The hunt gives the hell of a lot of men a way to support their families. And most of those men are mad keen on hunting so they love their work. They have a lovely life. They are out all day following the hounds. I know a lot of fence-menders and – I promise you – none of those fellows would do anything different. I don't know what those bloody anti's want those men to do. Do they want them sitting around smoking pot on the dole?'

The hunt provides much other esoteric employment. It gives work to the makers of special hunting diaries, in which the huntsman can look up where all the meets will be held in the future season. A hunting diary has pages on which the owner can jot down every move that the fox made and every move that he and his horse made when following the hounds on a particular day. In his old age he re-reads his old hunting diaries with nostalgia.

The clothes of the hunt alone provide an important source of employment. They allow the British boot-maker to flourish. A pair of good modern hunting boots now costs up to £400. The riders need to buy themselves several pairs, for they tend to get scratched very soon. Any chic huntsman will have a special pair for the hunt balls just as he will have a special and lighter-weight hunting coat for the hunt's indoor activities. He gets far too hot if he tries to dance in a garment designed to keep him warm in the coldest British weather, which contains a flannel lining to protect the expensive cloth tails of his coat from being soiled by the sweat of his horse.

One single button for a hunting coat now costs at least £3, and considerably more if the button is engraved with the emblem of the hunt that its owner supports. A good coat requires many buttons and they often get ripped off by branches to the button maker's gain.

The top-hat makers, the bowler-hat makers, the jockey-cap makers, all derive a thriving living from the hunt. So do the makers of breeches. A traditional pair of hunting breeches used to be made of cavalry twill, but now that hard-wearing material is very difficult to obtain. Frank Hall of Market Harborough is one of the leading hunting tailors in Great Britain today. He is the great 'Mr Pink' of modern times and has the royal warrant to make all Prince Charles's hunting coats. He is very distressed that he is now often forced to use inferior, surrogate materials. He told me that after the Second World War younger huntsmen and huntswomen started using a nylon material for their breeches. Lacking the maids who once worked all night getting the mud off the hunting breeches of their masters and mistresses, the younger sports people found synthetic materials easier to clean. This change in fashion proved disastrous for the makers of cavalry twill and the mill that produced it has now closed down.

The hunt provides a market for many curious little industries. The taxidermists who stuff the foxes' heads so they can be hung as trophies on the walls derive their main living from the hunt, as do those who turn the 'pads' or feet of foxes into paper weights. The Guild of Loriners (bit and spur makers) would be hard hit if the sport was ever abolished. The hunt supports the makers of whips and riding-crops. It takes Hilaire Belloc's instructions very seriously: 'It is the duty of the wealthy man to provide employment for the artisan.' The hunt takes on this duty. Only the huntsman requires a carved ivory handle for his whip. Who else needs an engraved silver top for his riding-crop or purchases a wooden device that helps with the removal of the sticky, sweaty hunting boot?

The equipment of the horses creates many more jobs. The farriers, the veterinarians, the girth makers, the horse-box and horse-rug makers, the stirrup makers, the bridle makers, the snaffle makers, the saddle makers, the saddle-sandwich-box makers, the martingale makers, the halter makers, the leading-rein makers, the list goes on and on, and all these makers of equestrian equipment have very good reason to be grateful to the hunt.

And there was certainly a feeling of gratitude amongst the followers of the Quorn on the day that I attended their meet. They were grateful to the riders not only because their sport helped to promote local prosperity, but because they had taken the trouble to put on such a dazzling sartorial display.

I wondered how long it had taken every individual rider to dress up to such a level of perfection. In the 1920s a huntswoman would take two hours to dress herself properly for a day's hunting. If she was planning to cub-hunt she had to rise very early indeed. Her maid would also get up at dawn to struggle with her mistress's breeches, for they had to be done up with button hooks and were worn skin-tight. If she was at all overweight, the donning of the breeches was an early-morning battle. Then there was the tying of the elaborate lawn 'stock', the pulling on of the boots. It was all immensely time-consuming.

The women riders of the Quorn may not have taken two hours to prepare themselves, but their appearance was so immaculate that it was unlikely such exquisiteness could have been achieved in haste. Their make-up alone looked as if it had taken lengthy preparation. Most of them wore a heavy, slightly orange foundation which was more suitable for the television studio and the stage than for the cold British outdoors. Examining them at close range at the meet, their stage-painted appearance with the heavily pencilled eyebrows and the purple and green eye-shadows looked a little overdone. But their maquillage was not intended to be examined closely. It was meant to have an impressionistic effect. It was a make-up that was highly effective from afar, and it worked most successfully when its wearers were galloping at full pace over the countryside.

The scarlet coat of the huntsman was originally chosen

because red is the colour that the human eye can best detect over long distances. It helps the huntsman's followers to discover where he is. The gaudy orange of the foundation cream on many of the faces of the women riders worked on much the same principle. It made them stand out when they were seen thundering across fields in the far distance. It gave them a healthy and glamorous look. It added a clever finishing touch to their lovely clothes.

The beautiful spectacle laid on by the Quorn was all the more poignant because, by the very nature of the sport, its beauty had to be fleeting. Once the hounds moved off, it wouldn't take many minutes before the perfect turn-out of every individual would be ruined. All those flawless white breeches would be splattered with flying mud. In the old days the boots of the huntsman used to be polished with champagne and apricots. This luxurious and spendthrift practice has now died out, but the Quorn hunting boots were still gleaming with a very high finish. Once the hounds drew their first fox many of those perfect boots would soon be scratched by hawthorn spikes. One scrape against a gate would tear the hide of the leather. Many of the hunting coats that had been cut from such expensive cloth would soon be horribly ripped by brambles and branches. The sheen of their lovely velvet collars would not be improved once it rained.

The horses and ponies who were about to hunt with the Quorn were so well-groomed that you could have used their flanks as mirrors. It looked as if the girl-grooms who work for the hunt had been up all night plaiting the manes, curry-combing the tails and blackening the hooves of these superb, prancing animals whose coats were a shining testament to the love that had gone into their grooming. The girl-grooms of Great Britain are amongst the most exploited minorities that these islands produce. Many of them work half the night without receiving any overtime. They are accustomed to rising at around five-thirty in the morning, and receive about £30 a week for their labours.

Philip Larkin felt that it would be impossible to organise a successful writers' strike because most writers only wanted to get on with their writing. Like writers, many girl-grooms only want to go on with their profession. They never go on strike and their passion for working with horses makes them feel that their work is its own reward.

At the Quorn meet the labour of the slave girls of the stables shone out. It showed in the rippling coats of the horses and it sparkled in the impeccable state of the bridles, saddles and stirrups. It must have taken hours to get all that equestrian equipment into such pristine condition. And once the hunt was under way all these exquisitely turned out horses would be muddied within minutes, and at worst they could be bloodied. The meet was a splendid 'happening'. Its glory was intended to be transient.

The modern huntsman will say that he sees himself as the guest of the farmer. He takes his role as a guest very seriously. He arrives at the meet dressed with the same care that he would take if he were attending a fashionable dinner party. The attention that he pays to his glamorous attire is intended as a gesture of gratitude and deference towards his host. The farmer who'd lent his fields to the Quorn on the day that I went car-hunting might have felt peeved in the evening when he examined the state of his fences. But when he looked at his guests as they assembled to drink their stirrup cups he certainly could not have felt that they had dishonoured him by any impropriety of dress.

'All traditional,' sighed Jimmy Herbert as he gazed at the equestrian group that was parading before us. 'Nothing untraditional,' he whispered with happy wonderment.

He told me that some young girls occasionally tried to break away from traditional forms of hunting attire and improve upon it, but the results were often calamitous.

'Last season I saw a young girl turn up to hunt with the Fernie and you couldn't believe what she was wearing . . . She had on these big shiny earrings and I suppose that she thought she looked very special and all the fellows would fancy her!' Jimmy gave a knowing huntsman's laugh.

'Well, the silly girl had hardly hunted for an hour before one of her earrings got caught in a branch and her horse went galloping on and she lost the lobe of her ear. It was torn right off her.' Jimmy shook his head reprovingly.

He told me that all hunting clothes were worn for a reason. The hair-nets worn by all the women prevented their hair from getting entangled in trees. 'Look at those stocks,' he said. He pointed at the white cravats that were round the necks of the women riders. 'They can unwind those stocks if someone has an accident,' he said. 'Those stocks make a very good bandage, they have got a lot of material in them. And you see those tie-pins they are all wearing . . . Well, they come in very handy if you need to make a tourniquet. They can use those tie-pins to keep the bandage tight.'

I hadn't realised that the concept of the inevitable accident had been incorporated in the hunting clothing.

I'd read in a local newspaper that Prince Charles had recently appeared on the hunting field with a piece of pink elastic round his chin. At first I'd assumed that this report was an invention of the media, but I'd checked out the rumour with Rupert Smith-Ryland, who is one of the keenest huntsmen in Great Britain.

'I'm afraid that he did,' he'd said to me ruefully. 'But the wonderful thing is Prince Charles loves hunting so much. That's all that really matters.'

I could only imagine that when Prince Charles went hunting with his riding hat secured by a piece of pink elastic he'd done it as a joke. Purist fox-hunters would prefer to see a huntsman turn up at the meet naked than to see him arrive with any form of elastic securing his hat.

If a rider's hat needs securing so that it won't fly off when its owner gallops, it means that it has not been properly made by an expensive hatter. The hunting community's horror of white elastic is one of their most ingrained snobberies. As for pink elastic . . . It is unlikely that many fashionable huntsmen would have been aware of the very existence of quite such a degrading and repulsive substance. So what could they have felt when they saw it round the chin of their future King?

I examined every rider at the Quorn meet to see if any of them had decided to copy Prince Charles's audacious example. Every chin that I looked at was free from elastic.

I admired the Prince for his humorous violation of one of the most holy laws of the British hunting field. He'd found the most original way to be 'in the pink'.

# 16

# The Old-Timers

*'The first pursuit a young man just out of boyhood should take up is hunting and afterwards he should go on to other branches of education. Hunting improves the sight and hearing and keeps men from growing old . . .'*

Xenophon

When I attended the Quorn meet as a car-hunting observer, I was interested to watch the tough, resolute little children who were twirling round in the most dangerous fashion on their tiny bucking ponies. Unlike Molly Keane's fictional characters they had no tears streaming down their cheeks. They were more like the children of the Dukes of Somerset. Their parents would have to limit their hunting days if they didn't want to spoil them.

They seemed very brave, these young hunting children, and their parents were equally brave to allow them to enter what Prince Charles has described as the 'Cavalry Charge' of the Quorn, where they could so easily be jumped on and trampled.

There were also a number of old people amongst the riders, their hair looking brilliantly white in contrast to the blackness of their top hats and bowlers. They too seemed courageous to risk old bones that might not heal very well if they were broken.

After the age of fifty the nerve of many huntsmen starts to

go. But long ago these old Quorn followers had overcome their midlife crisis. Their stamina in staying with their beloved sport had rendered them immune to many of the problems that can beset the aged. They were not in a situation where they sat at home feeling pointless and lonely and finished, but had made themselves so self-sufficient that it mattered to them very little if they were neglected by their children.

Until they sustained some unlucky injury they enjoyed exceptionally good health. All the hours of exercise that they took in the fresh air kept them exceedingly fit. The cheeks of the elderly riders of the Quorn were childishly scarlet without the effect of make-up.

Having lived for fox-hunting and refused retirement, their lives were just as full of thrill and challenge as they had been when they were young. At the end of their days they continued to enjoy all the pleasures of a pursuit that many people have found more rewarding and long-lasting than sex.

A London barrister, whose mother hunted until she was in her seventies, had described to me the way she now copes with the vicissitudes of her old age.

'Mother was fine all through her fifties, sixties and most of her seventies. She was a widow, but I never had to worry about her. I hardly heard from her. She was too busy with all her hunting. She was always in a horse-box going off to some meet. She was as happy as a bee . . . Then when Mother was seventy-five she had this awful fall. Her horse caught its foot in a rabbit hole and it did a sort of somersault and it came crashing down on top of her. Her spine and her hip were badly injured and her doctors told her she must never hunt again.'

The barrister said that he'd assumed at first his mother would die very soon, he couldn't imagine how she would survive. However, her injuries healed to a point – she was very tough physically, and soon managed to limp around. He had then only really worried about her morale. What would she do with her life? He had feared she would die from lack of function and incentive.

The old lady turned out to be far more resourceful than he had imagined. She took up hunting by telephone. At the end of the day she now lies in bed and makes phone calls to her hunting friends all over the British Isles. She makes them describe their day in minute detail. She follows their horses stride by stride. They tell her where they first 'drew' a fox. They tell her exactly where it headed – where it went to ground. As she knows the terrains of all the hunting counties in Great Britain extremely well, if she is told that the hounds 'found' at Spinney Covert, and then headed left towards Cherry Farm, she can see every field the riders galloped through. She knows every jump and gate and obstacle that they must have encountered. She can lie back on her pillows while her friends provide her with thrilling hunts which she relives in her brain. They are so vivid to her that she might be watching them on a video. She gets almost as much joy out of reconstructing all the chases from which she is debarred, than if she was still on a horse following the hounds in person.

The barrister told me that his mother is still an immensely popular figure in the modern British hunting community. Many huntsmen and huntswomen have a longing to recount the details of the vicissitudes and triumphs that they have met with during their pursuit of the fox. They often find it hard to get listeners. Even their fellow huntsmen are not always keen to lend an ear.

'Mother does want to listen. They love her for that. They can be as tedious as they want to with her. She doesn't find their hunting tales boring at all.'

The barrister felt that in a sense his mother was now hunting even more than she'd done in her youth. By getting such detailed telephonic reports from all over the British Isles, she could hunt with more packs of hounds – and all on the same day.

'Mother rings up one of her friends and they can make her

feel that she's been hunting with the Meynell. She'll know exactly what all the prevailing scents have been. She'll know precisely where a fox was lost and why. She'll get quite angry apportioning the blame. Having had a splendid day with the Meynell, she'll telephone a friend who has just finished a day's hunting with the Belvoir. She'll then vicariously follow all their runs. Mother's life is as good as it can be at present,' the barrister had told me. He had then added in the mildly bitter and sarcastic tone that many children of hunting mothers adopt when describing the lifestyle of passionate huntresses. 'Mother is in at the "kill" so many times a day now. I honestly think that her life has never been so good.'

Watching the old-timers prancing on their gleaming horses at the Quorn meet, I thought of the barrister's mother. By the end of the day would some of these snowy-headed riders be forced by ill fate to become telephone-hunters? There was no telling: just as there was no certainty that all the children and the horses would return unscathed to their homes that evening. Some might not return at all. And it was that possibility that gave a festive feeling to the assembly, like playing Russian roulette. Drink your port and enjoy it, for – who knows – it might well be your last. None of the riders – not even the experienced master, the competent huntsman and his whipper-in – could feel confident that destiny might not single him out and present him with the black ace from the pack.

This sense of shared threat produced a mood of solidarity and joy which was infectious. It spread to the grooms and the fence-menders, horse-box drivers and the car-hunters, the boys on motor-bikes and the people who followed the hunt on foot and on bicycles. We all felt that we were in something very important together. A battle was on and it had to be waged. As to the validity of this battle, there was no one to dispute it. And when the huntsman blasted a clarion call on his horn and the riders moved off, it seemed irrelevant to question why quite so many people should have gathered themselves together in order to bring about the demise of one small fox.

Once we were hunting in earnest, I learned from Jimmy Herbert that the pleasure he got from the sport was very different from mine. He didn't like going to meets. They were not the part of the hunting ritual that he enjoyed. He had only attended the Quorn meet out of kindness to me, and because he'd felt that a novice car-hunter ought to see the 'cream' at close range. Normally he only joined the hunt after the hounds had 'found'. He followed exactly the same routines as Prince Charles. It was the hunting that he adored. All the foreplay and the hanging around drinking stirrup cups bored him.

As we drove along or, more precisely, as we did the car-huntsman's horrible slow chuff down the chaotic, traffic-burdened lanes, he explained what attracted him to the hunt. I had not realised the goals of a car-hunter differed quite steeply from those of the mounted huntsman, and had assumed that car-hunting was a continuation of horseback hunting by other means. But this was only partially true.

Jimmy Herbert didn't want to kill any foxes. 'I hope that they won't kill today,' he said. He hated it when they dug a fox out of the ground. If a fox was clever enough to find a spot to hide in when the hunt had arranged that every hole for miles around be blocked up by human earth-stoppers, he felt that the fox should win. Everyone should take off their hats to that intelligent animal and it should be allowed to go free. He couldn't see that it was sporting to dig out a trapped animal. The hunt could always go in pursuit of a new fox. It was boring for the riders, even worse for the car-hunters, when the terrier men started coming in with their spades and their dogs. The whole procedure usually took them hours. He was certain that many riders agreed with him (particularly the women), but unfortunately the farmers blackmailed the hunt. They refused to allow their fields to be used for hunting unless they had some guarantee that the hounds would destroy any fox that they found.

Jimmy Herbert told me that in all his years of car-hunting,

he'd never once been present at a 'digging out'. He refused to watch that. Fortunately most of the nasty part of hunting took place in thick woods impossible to reach by car. He'd never been forced to witness it.

'Foxes really are clever animals,' he said. 'They are just as clever as they are meant to be.'

He told me that there was a farmer who lived near his village who was violently opposed to blood sports. He owned quite a few acres and refused to allow the hounds on his land.

'It's a joke,' Jimmy said. 'Whenever the hunt goes anywhere near that man's land, his fields start filling up with foxes. Sometimes I've driven past that fellow's farm and I've never seen so many foxes in my whole life. They just sit there in his fields and they stay there until the hounds go home. The vixens bring all the cubs. They make the whole thing look like a family outing. I always have to laugh when I see them all . . . Sometimes I think they are laughing too . . . You see the hunt would get sued if they tried to chase them on that land. You wouldn't think that foxes would know that, but somehow they do!'

The point of hunting for Jimmy was to see a fox running and it was the point for most car-hunters. I had not understood this when I'd gone out with the Pytchley.

As the hounds scoured the countryside they scared up foxes and the frightened animals would often run towards the car-hunters who were gathered in their traffic-jam. The person who first spotted the fox running across open ground became the hero of the car-hunt. They would scream 'halloas' and wave a white handkerchief. It was as if they had scored a goal. Later they celebrated their 'viewing' in the local pubs.

Jimmy kept drawing my attention to the drivers of other vehicles. He told me that they were brilliant huntsmen. Last week, out hunting with the Cottesmore, some of these men had apparently spotted as many as five foxes – and all on the same day.

The skill of the game for the car-hunters was to position

your car in a place where you felt you were most likely to get a viewing of a fox in flight. Jimmy insisted this was an art. You had to work out the position of the hounds and calculate the direction in which they were likely to drive the animal. You had to manoeuvre your car through the hazards of the traffic so that you could be standing in a field waiting to view the fox as it ran.

We had not been car-hunting for more than a few minutes before we saw the first bleeding victim of the sport.

A man in a red coat and a black velvet jockey cap came along a lane on foot leading his horse past all the cars. His horse had a leg that was in a hideous condition. It had been badly ripped on some fence and all the white bone from its knee to its hoof was exposed. The leg of a thoroughbred horse is fine and delicate. Any injury inflicted on something so thin and quivering is a sickening sight.

'Silly idiot,' Jimmy Herbert said. 'Look what he's done to his poor horse. That animal will have to be put down . . . '

Jimmy didn't seem to like huntsmen. He only liked the hunt. 'Some of these huntsmen are real brutes,' he said. 'Last week when I was out hunting with the Cottesmore, I saw a man kill his horse. He was a huge fat fellow – he must have weighed way over eighteen stone. He was riding this poor little mare. She was only about fifteen hands. It was ridiculous. She wasn't nearly up to his weight. I don't know what that fool was doing riding her . . . But she dropped down dead right under him. I watched it with my own two eyes. And it wasn't a pretty sight. And the stupid rider didn't give a damn. He was asking everyone to get him a new horse. That was all that great fat man cared about. Most car-hunters take much more care of their cars than some of the huntsmen take of their horses.'

Jimmy Herbert was one of the best drivers I had ever seen. His control of his little car was amazing – he could make it turn in the smallest of areas, and could reverse it at the highest speed. His car seemed like a performing circus animal, he knew how to make it dance and pirouette on its back wheels.

He bypassed cars that blocked our passage by making a daring use of ditches. I soon understood why his car was so scratched and battered – he used it as if he were driving a tank. We went zooming down the steepest of inclines and splashed along in deep mud and water. Because he used it like a tank it seemed to acquire many of the capabilities of a tank. On the occasions when we took short cuts over stony fields and hit a particularly hard object, the car would jump in the air as if it was dancing in pain. A terrible smell of burning eggs exuded from its engine. But Jimmy Herbert's car never seemed to stall.

Every time we came to a gate or a gap in the hedges, Jimmy made me get out and we both went and stood in a field. I soon started to find this getting in and out of the car an exhausting and unbearable procedure. I dreaded every gate that we came to. I knew he would make me get out. It was a bitterly cold day and I was not correctly dressed as he was in warm and appropriate car-hunter's garb.

I found it dismal standing on windy hill-tops, while Jimmy scoured the countryside with his binoculars. He seemed heated by the excitement of the chase. He didn't feel the cold at all. He was mad keen to view a fox. I would have preferred to see the horses jumping, but it took a long time for either of us to get what we wanted. I stood shivering beside him and we stared out at an expanse of bleak wintry countryside. I wondered why he wanted to see a fox so much. Was he trying to outdo the hounds by spotting a prey that they had missed?

It seemed to me that you could see a fox any day of the year. If you stationed yourself on a hill and waited long enough, by the law of averages you would probably see a fox in the end. It didn't seem necessary to follow the Quorn to see one.

'My late wife was barren,' Jimmy suddenly said to me. 'That was a great sadness for both of us. We tried and tried – but nothing happened.'

I discovered that conversation came in fits and spurts when you car-hunted with a companion. Sometimes you were not meant to speak at all because it disturbed your driver's concentration. But during the *longueurs* when there was no action at all, the fact that you were driving and driving in a no man's land without a specific destination gave you a sense of unreality which removed social constraints and conversation became intimate.

'My wife and I used to do a lot of fostering,' Jimmy said to me. Because we were both out hunting and everyone we met was totally involved with hunting, I was slow to understand what he meant. I thought for a moment that he was using a hunting term. 'Fostering' sounded like something connected with hounds.

'We used to take in quite a few black ones,' Jimmy said. 'Most people don't like to take in the coloureds. But my wife and I – we couldn't see the difference. Black or white – they were all kids to us. Some of them had funny names, Ezekiel, Infanta, Zachariah. But they were lovely children and we never had any trouble with any of them. In the winter we just used to pack up some sandwiches and we'd pop them in the back of the car and we'd take them out fox-hunting. You couldn't believe how much they loved it. They all became mad-keen little fox-hunters. It was beautiful to see it . . . '

Jimmy said that his foster children were all grown now and they were scattered all over different parts of England. But they often came to see him at Christmas and he always tried to give them a good day with the hounds.

'They send me postcards all the time,' Jimmy said. 'Keep up the good hunting, Dad. That's what they always write to me!'

At one point Jimmy pointed out a figure who had stationed himself on the top of a haystack that had been constructed on a high ridge. This man had chosen a very cunning spot from which he could get a commanding view over the whole countryside. He made an ink-black, rather sinister, silhouette against the grey sky, feverishly scouring the surrounding terrain with his field glasses. He seemed vigilant as an admiral searching the seas for enemy ships.

'I bet you think that's a car-hunter.' Jimmy Herbert laughed at my ignorance. 'That man is not looking for a fox.'

The watcher on the haystack was apparently a wary farmer. He would remain sitting on his vantage point until nightfall when the hounds returned to their kennels. As he owned the surrounding fields he was keeping a very strict binoculared eye on the damage that was being inflicted on his fences. He was going to see to it that the fence-menders did their job, and if any gates were left open and his cattle escaped, he would make certain that he received ample financial reparation from the hunt.

'The Quorn are extremely rich,' Jimmy said, 'they have so many subscribers. They are also very clever – they publish a list of the sums of money that their supporters have donated to the hunt in the course of the year. Nobody wants it to be known that they've given a miserable little sum to the Quorn. I think they've found a very good way to get the proper support that they need.'

Jimmy ran into a lot of car-hunting friends as we hung around in various gloomy ploughed English fields that contained buried turnips. They propounded their various theories as to where a fox was most likely to head. If the hounds entered the little wood at Dingley from the south, the fox would head out north towards Thurloe Ridge. They all spoke with the confidence of experts.

We rushed back into our cars and headed to the spot that the most knowing followers of this peculiar sport had selected from their years of experience. Jimmy insisted that there was great skill in the prediction of where a fox would run at any particular point. He was adamant in his claim that certain car-hunters were much better huntsmen than others. There were quite a lot of ancient men on bicycles following the Quorn, many of whom were over eighty, he said. He considered them to be the best huntsmen in the non-riding hunting field. They had so much experience. They had been hunting since they were sixteen, and always saw more foxes than anyone.

Although we took endless skilled advice we never seemed to see a fox, and I soon ceased to believe that there was any skill to the sport of car-hunting. If you spotted a fox – or if you failed to spot a fox – it all seemed to be luck.

Finally Jimmy Herbert viewed a fox. He gave a scream of triumph and he waved his handkerchief.

'Look at him! Look at him!' he shouted. 'Can you see him? He's down there in the valley.'

I couldn't see a fox, I was too short-sighted. Jimmy thrust his binoculars into my hand. I looked through them and they were out of focus.

'Do you see that clump of oaks?' Jimmy said. 'He's going to the left of that clump.'

I couldn't see the clump and I couldn't see the fox. I made a stupid mistake – I should have pretended that I could see it. The pretence might have spared me many more hours of painful car-hunting.

Jimmy took my failure to see the fox as a personal failure and it made him resolute. 'We are not stopping until you see a fox,' he said. 'I've set my heart on that.'

Unfortunately we never saw another one. Jimmy kept me out car-hunting until it was so late and so dark that it became farcical. No one could have seen a fox under such conditions. But he now seemed so happy, and had been so depressed at the start of the day, that I felt that it would be an act of cruelty if I were to beg him to stop. We went careering round lanes which had become deserted because our fellow car-hunters had gone home. We hadn't heard or seen the hounds for ages. I assumed that they had long ago 'packed in'. Jimmy didn't seem to care that now we weren't followers of the Quorn. He was no longer pursuing a sport that was peripheral to an older sport. His own game had become central and he pursued it with gusto and enormous pleasure.

I became more and more miserable, and increasingly bored,

exhausted and cold. I was also very hungry, but he wouldn't let me eat my sandwiches. 'We can't stop and eat while we are hunting,' he said quite crossly.

Normally he seemed to be very kind and considerate, but all that ceased once he was caught up in the thrills of his own particular form of chase.

At one point I thought I would scream if he didn't let me stop car-hunting and go home. But I still felt unable to tell him I was longing to stop. Such an admission still seemed too damping, discourteous and unkind. I continued to be false and compliant and enthusiastic. I disguised my misery. Inwardly I was cursing myself. Why hadn't I pretended that I could see the fox that had run by the clump of oaks?

'You know something,' Jimmy suddenly said. 'It's a real pleasure to go hunting with you. You have to hunt with someone who is really keen. My wife was a mad-keen hunter. I miss hunting with her so much. I find it very lonely hunting alone. It's been such a pleasure having you with me today.'

He looked very unhappy, his sense of loss had returned. I felt guilty and fraudulent. My role had become unpleasant. I was acting as a replacement for his adored dead wife when I secretly hated car-hunting.

'I'm sorry you didn't have a good day,' he said as we finally drove home.

'I enjoyed myself very much,' I lied.

'But you didn't have a good day. No one has a good day unless they see a fox. I really tried for you. I've hardly ever tried so hard in my whole life.'

'But I promise you that I didn't mind not seeing a fox.' I was being truthful as I tried to reassure him. Jimmy Herbert didn't like my attitude. I saw that I'd unwittingly offended him. He felt I *should* have minded having had quite such a bad day.

'I'll tell you something,' he said, 'the Melton Mowbray are meeting on Thursday. I'd really like to take you out hunting with them. I'd really like you to see a fox.'

'Oh no . . . ' I thought. I can't spend another miserable,

boring day, this time chasing after the Melton Mowbray. If I'm not careful, I'll spend the rest of the winter car-hunting with Jimmy Herbert.

I coughed, and I hedged, and I murmured that I had appointments on Thursday.

Jimmy started to lose all his boyish ebullience as we got near to home. He became increasingly melancholy. The drug of car-hunting was wearing off. He was returning to loneliness and bereavement and a wretched spartan meal of cheese. If fox-hunting was legally abolished, what would happen to this lonely man, I wondered.

'You know the only good thing in my life at the moment,' Jimmy Herbert spoke with bitterness as he dropped me off at my door, 'I only have to pay the electricity bill for *one side* of my double electric blanket.'

# 17

# The Retired Master

*'Not in the shouts and plaudits of the throng*
*but in ourselves are triumph and defeat.'*

Longfellow

Colonel Hignet is now eighty-six. He was the Master of the Pytchley Hounds for twenty years.

When I interviewed him, I was not imitating Professor Eysenck and trying to glean his attitudes towards capitalism and adultery, although the Colonel might have been very fascinating on those incendiary subjects. I was interested to hear about the unusual profession that he had taken up when a nasty fall on his head forced him to retire from the hunting field. When Colonel Hignet heard from his doctors that he must give up the sport to which he'd devoted his life, he took an audacious step and appointed himself as the 'Field Master' to the traffic that follows the Pytchley.

The role of the Field Master within the traditional hunt is very important. He is a hunt servant ranked below the Master of Fox-hounds, but he is entrusted with the responsibility of seeing that individual riders comport themselves properly on the field. He has to check to see that gates are not left open, and prevent hounds and young crops from being trampled. The Field Master protects the image of the hunt and does his best to see that the sport retains its popularity in the countryside.

Having driven with the unruly and idiosyncratic traffic that follows the Pytchley, I felt that when the Colonel had tried to 'Field Master' it he had taken on a very great challenge.

In his appearance, Colonel Hignet epitomises the ideal of the English gentleman. At eighty-six he is slim, energetic and handsome. With his excellent physique he mocks the health freaks and modern dietitians. He lives almost entirely on sugar. Not for the Colonel are any of the unrefined medically approved sugars. He likes the proper, delicious refined sugars that he enjoyed in his boyhood.

When I interviewed him, he drank a cup of coffee, but it was only coffee in name. It was really a large mug of coffee-flavoured sugar. The Colonel starts his day with something sweet, continues to eat and drink sugar products all through the day and has a last sweet snack before retiring to bed.

'I know they say that sugar is so bad for you,' he said, 'but I think it's all a lot of nonsense. Here I am . . . I feel perfectly well. I've got all my own teeth. What more do they want from a person of eighty-six?'

When I asked him about his Field Mastership of the Pytchley traffic, he said that it had been calamitous. The task had defeated him. He had very soon resigned.

'You couldn't do a thing with most of those drivers. I could master the Pytchley hounds, but I couldn't master those car-hunters. If you gave them an order, they just drove away and ignored you.'

Colonel Hignet said that although the car-hunters had refused to be Field Mastered, he was very grateful that they existed. 'They raised ten thousand pounds for the hunt last year. That's a hell of a lot of money. And for that, I say God bless them!'

'How did they manage to raise so much money?' I asked.

They had got hold of some walking sticks with a fox's head carved on their handles, and had auctioned these sticks at various hunt balls.

'People paid hundreds of pounds for those sticks once they'd had a few drinks,' the Colonel said. 'Some of those car-hunters have very ingenious ideas.'

Colonel Hignet told me when he had become a traffic Field

Master, he hadn't been forbidden to hunt altogether. 'The doctors said I could go on if I rode on some stupid old cob. I could only go five miles an hour! Well . . . ,' he said, 'I was used to being up at the front. Five miles an hour wasn't good enough for me.'

Knowing that he could only feel humiliated and frustrated if he hunted on an old cob, the Colonel had decided to give up hunting altogether. Years ago, when he was doing military service in India, he'd contracted some oriental disease of the liver. He'd been told that he would never drink again.

'I can't even have a sherry,' he told me. 'But hunting and drinking – it's much the same thing. If you have to give them up – you give them up. There is no point in sitting around moaning and saying your life is finished.'

The Colonel now uses sugar as a substitute for alcohol, and he'd hoped that if he acted as Field Master to the traffic that follows the Pytchley hounds, he would find the task a satisfying substitute for fox-hunting. He'd originally thought that he would be quite suited to the job, for, unlike most huntsmen, he has no horror and mistrust of machines.

'Most huntsmen really loathe machines. They don't even want you to know how to fix a bicycle. They hate you to know anything about engines and all that.'

He felt that this loathing of machines had been responsible for the amazing step that the British government had taken in 1939. When Great Britain had first declared war on Germany, the government had instantly issued an order that every hunting horse in the country was to become the automatic property of the army.

'They couldn't change their anti-machine mentality,' the Colonel said. 'You wouldn't have thought that anyone could believe that the last war would be fought on horseback – but somehow they did. They'd seen what happened to the cavalry in the First World War – but they didn't take it in.'

In 1939, when the government requisitioned all the hunting horses, it led to peculiar situations. Huntsmen hid their horses in their billiard rooms and wine-cellars. Many British horses remained in the most eccentric hiding places for the entire duration of the war.

'People didn't like the idea of their horses competing with German bombers and tanks,' the Colonel said. 'It wasn't lack of patriotism. They just felt that the government was going too far.'

Colonel Hignet had found that his acceptance of the machine was of little use when he'd tried to Field Master the vehicles that hunt with the Pytchley hounds.

'Some of the car-hunters are so irresponsible you couldn't believe it,' he said. 'It's tragic . . . They love the hunt so much and they do it so much harm. They give it a terrible name.'

Colonel Hignet had been very distressed by the way that some of the drivers would get out of their cars and leave them in a lane. They would go off and station themselves in a field with their binoculars.

'And they leave their engines running!' he said. 'It's perfectly horrible to watch them. All those fumes coming out of their cars . . . Can you imagine what that does to the scent?'

He made himself another mug of refined sugar, and after he'd drunk it he managed to look slimmer and younger and healthier than before he'd consumed yet another dose of the dietitian's poison. I felt that he knew how to surmount the latent dangers of sugar in much the same way that he'd surmounted the obstacles of the hunting field when he'd mastered the Pytchley hounds in his youth.

Talking with the Colonel, sugar and war and hunting kept weaving through our conversation as if they were all interchangeable. One thing led to another. He told me that he had been David Niven's Commanding Officer in the Second World War.

'Splendid fellow, David. But what a killer! You'd never think it when you look at him playing those smooth, charming, debonair characters in all those Hollywood movies. But David was a killer! David liked to kill two Germans before breakfast. I've never seen anything like it. He was a man who really loved to run his bayonet through the belly!'

The Colonel said that the Second World War had been a dirty war and David Niven had played it dirty.

'David never took any prisoners,' he said. 'David wasn't having any of that. We were on a boat once and I remember David just shoving prisoners overboard.'

He said that David Niven had been amazing. He had been making a fortune in Hollywood playing the lead in all those 1930s comedies, but the second that England declared war on Germany he was on the next boat back to Europe and had joined Colonel Hignet's regiment. 'It's amazing, don't you think?' Colonel Hignet asked me.

I was feeling amazed and a little queasy, wondering how we had meandered so easily from the subject of Field Mastering the Pytchley car followers, to this unexpected and repulsive vignette. But the Colonel got us back to our subject without any abrupt transition. He suddenly asked me if I had read Surtees and quoted me a passage. The creator of Jorrocks is the huntsman's Shakespeare, and the Colonel could recite him by heart.

In the passage he chose to quote to me, Jorrocks shouts at another rider, '"Hold hard, you hairdresser on the chestnut horse!"

"Hairdresser, Sir! I am an officer in the 91st regiment."

"Then you officer in the 91st regiment, wot looks like a hairdresser, hold hard!" rejoined Mr Jorrocks, trotting on.'

'I'm afraid you can't behave like Jorrocks with the car-hunters,' the Colonel said. 'It simply doesn't work.'

# 18

# The Case for Drag-Hunting

*'To hunt without killing is like having sexual intercourse without orgasm.'*
Montaigne

Robert Churchward, who died in 1981, was the joint Master of the Shropshire Fox-hounds. There has probably never been a master like him. For forty years he devoted his life to hunting. He hunted stags with the Devon and Somerset Stag-hounds, he shot jaguars, bears, tapirs, peccaries and deer, and hunted with twenty different British packs including the Quorn, the Fernie, the Meynell, the Atherstone, the North and South Cheshire, with Sir Watkin Wynn's, the Hampshire, the Crawley and Horsham and the Vine. He also hunted in the United States. In April, when the fox-hunting season ended, Robert Churchward took the job of whipper-in to the Staffordshire otter hounds. He arranged his life so that there was not a month in the year when he was deprived of the opportunity to kill some animal.

Then, after forty years of uninterrupted hunting, he suddenly gave it up. He was unique as a Master of Fox-hounds, and would have been a misfit in Professor Eysenck's statistical survey of typical masters, for he suddenly denounced the sport to which his life had been dedicated.

He caused consternation in fox-hunting circles because he wrote a little booklet entitled *The Master of Hounds Speaks*, in which he revealed practices which the hunting community had always kept secret.

The conversion of Robert Churchward was like a religious conversion. He openly challenged the late Duke of Beaufort's defence of the sport, maintaining that his own hunting experience was every bit as extensive. The Duke always claimed that it was less cruel to hunt a fox with hounds than to allow it to be trapped or poisoned by farmers. Churchward felt that trapping and poisoning were not the only alternatives to fox-hunting. A skilled marksman could provide the animal with an instant, clean death. It could be spared all the agony and terror that it experiences before being torn to bits by the teeth of the hounds.

Robert Churchward started his hunting career at the age of six. He described his first day out with the hounds:

> I will never forget that crisp November day when my father's groom took me to a meet of the Meynell hunt on the borders of Leicestershire. It was thrilling. I had no idea what was in store – how could I have? My eyes almost popped out of my head when I saw a fox running out of cover. I galloped on over hedges and across brooks doing my best to keep up with the hounds. It seemed to me that we must have covered hundreds of miles. Then almost as suddenly as we'd started, we stopped. A fox had run up a steep grass embankment at the side of a country lane.
>
> As I coaxed my pony up to the fast-growing circle of sweating horses and shouting men and women I saw, in one second, a bedraggled vixen baring its teeth, and in the next second an explosion of fur and flesh as the leading hounds fell upon it.
>
> Everybody was cheering wildly. I wanted to cheer too, so that my father's friends would know I was enjoying our 'victory'. But my eyes were fixed on the place where the hounds were snapping at the brown, blood-drenched body of the vixen.

As the animal's flesh was torn away I caught the flash of white, glossy bone.

I was sickened at the sight of the mangled flesh. Yet I was strangely thrilled. It was horrible to kill a defenceless animal. Yet its pursuit and slaughter had clearly given joyous sport to many people.

If ever a boy needed moral guidance it was I at that moment. A few words from an adult expressing compassion for the tortured animal would have turned me against fox-hunting for ever.

But the only words I heard were calculated to play on my boyish pride in the chase.

'You're a lucky young man,' said my father's groom as he rode over to where I was waiting. 'First time out and a kill.' His face was flushed with exultation.

It was a clear invitation to revel in the spectacle of slaughter. And – what else could a boy of six do? – I accepted it.

From that day onwards fox-hunting was my joy. I believed it to be the greatest sport ever invented by man.

I began to learn all I could about it, to master all its customs and traditions.

Robert Churchward's little pamphlet was to make him violently unpopular. It is a rare document. Very few committed huntsmen have tried to take an objective view of their experiences on the hunting field. He gave a chilling description of a hunt that he attended when he was a boy of thirteen:

On rounding a sharp bend in the road, I had a clear and close view of a nearly beaten fox.

It dragged itself slowly and painfully through the blackthorn hedge and squeezed wearily under the gate on the other side of the road. The animal was a lightly-built vixen and was obviously reaching the end of its tether.

With ears laid back to catch the sound of pursuit, it

> tottered a few steps into the field, trailing its bedraggled brush along the ground.
>
> Its eyes were glazed and its tongue lolled out. Then it sank, exhausted, into a plough furrow, its breath coming in great heaving gasps.
>
> Suddenly I became aware of the approach of hounds. They rounded the side of the wood in full cry. Staccato toots of the hunting horn and the beat and thud of the horses' hooves echoed all around me.
>
> Round the bend they came and into the field. Now the fox was in the hounds' full view.
>
> Their cries rose in triumph. The leading hounds flung themselves on to the half-dead fox, seizing it wherever they could get a grip with their fangs.
>
> Each late arrival leaped into the middle of the circle of death in a frantic effort to get a grip on the fox. Sometimes a hound got hold of another hound in the frenzy. Yelps of pain added to the macabre turmoil.
>
> The huntsman jumped off his horse, he waded into the whirling mêlée striking the hounds with his whip and shouting, 'Garn! Leave it!!', a cry that is heard at every kill, the object being to preserve the mask, pads, and brush of the fox so that they can be presented to deserving riders.

Young Churchward watched the huntsman chop off the head of the fox with a skilful twist of the knife. The man chopped off the brush and pads. He threw the remains of the bleeding carcass in the air, shouting, 'Tear 'im and eat 'im!'

Robert Churchward then heard an irritable bellow behind him. 'Open that bloody gate and be damned quick about it!' The master had arrived late for the kill. His face was the colour of a ripe mulberry because a gate was preventing him from fulfilling his duties.

The thirteen-year-old Churchward quickly opened the gate and to his embarrassment the master stared at him and asked if he was the son of General Churchward. 'Are you the boy who has been coming out regularly with us all season?'

Robert Churchward stammered and he admitted that he was. 'Then it's about time you were blooded!' shouted the master.

Churchward was then forced to submit to the ritual very similar to that which James II used to inflict on his courtiers.

'I stood still,' wrote Churchward, 'the huntsman came towards me with the fox's brush. The master brought it up to my face, smearing me with the wet, bloodstained stump, still with the traces of excrement clinging to it. I must have flinched because I heard someone say, "Stand still boy. And take it like a man."'

The master then stepped back and admired his own handiwork. He told Churchward to go home and keep the blood and excrement on his face. He was to go down to dinner without washing it off so that his father, the General, could be proud of him.

'Hunt members crowded round to congratulate me,' Robert Churchward wrote. 'I rode off alone, half-proud of my initiation but inwardly nauseated by it.'

General Churchward was predictably proud of his son, who never admitted that he'd had any qualms or reservations about the splendour of his recent experience.

James II always forbade his courtiers to wash off the blood and guts of all the stags with which he liked to smear them. When young Churchward displayed gore as a proof of his valour, he was following many an historic precedent.

The qualms that he felt on feeling the wet, smelling stump of the amputated brush of the fox as it was rubbed on his face lay dormant for the next thirty years. Then after he'd spent half a lifetime dedicating himself to every form of hunting an incident occurred which revived them.

'We were hunting a particularly stubborn fox,' he wrote. 'There was a long chase; finally the fox went to ground and it took us three hours to dig him out. When we finally found him, the reason for his courage became obvious, he was trying to shield his mate and a litter of newborn cubs.'

The hounds eventually tore the vixen and her family to pieces and Churchward as Master of Hounds rode over to control the scene of the kill.

'It was then that a small boy approached me and said tearfully, "Please, mister, what shall I do with this? They've killed all the others." He held out a tiny cub; its eyes still shut like that of a kitten.'

'I was stunned,' wrote Churchward. 'For forty years I had been hunting foxes. Since I had become master and learned all the behind-the-scene secrets of hunting, I had begun to have serious doubts about it all. But nothing made so great an impression on me as this. Without a word I took the cub and pushed it into the pocket of my pink coat . . . '

Churchward took the cub back to his house and gave it to his young daughter. The cub soon became very tame and the family named it Toddy, but he continued fox-hunting, even though he had a tame fox-cub eating bread and milk in his sitting-room. Later he was to say that he felt ashamed that he hadn't given up hunting sooner. But finally he did and incurred the fury of the hunting community by writing his account of some of the unsavoury and unsporting tricks that he had witnessed during his mastership. He demolished the old hunting myth that the hunt only hunts on behalf of the farmer by confessing that during the height of his hunting career he used to transport, as was expected of him, litters of fox-cubs to the terrains of neighbouring hunts which were suffering from a shortage of foxes.

Out of fear that the anti-blood sport groups might discover his activities he always referred to the fox-cubs as 'roses'. 'I'm delivering a sack of roses,' he would say on the telephone, fearing that he might be overheard. He would then set off to plant the cubs in an artificial earth, which had been specially constructed so that they would prosper in its shelter.

He also revealed that it was a common practice for the hunt

to use 'bagged foxes'. A 'bagged' fox is caught the night before it is used for hunting. Its 'earth' is stopped up and the trapped animal is dug out of the ground and put in a bag.

Once the hunt is under way, a hunt servant slashes its 'pads' with a knife and it is secretly released in front of the hounds. Like the stags at the Elizabethan court the animal has no chance. The hounds pick up the scent of the blood that streams from its wounded feet. They catch it in a few minutes.

Churchward said that this unpleasant ritual was most often practised when a hunt had a visiting master or some other visiting dignitary that they wanted to impress.

I interviewed the widow of Robert Churchward, for I was curious to learn how the hunting community had reacted to the defection of one of their star masters. Mrs Churchward is an intelligent, attractive woman in her late sixties. She now lives alone in a flat in Windsor, and there are no hunting prints on her walls.

She herself was brought up in a hunting family. She said that it had taken her years to overcome her childhood indoctrination, just as it had taken her late husband years before he questioned the values he'd accepted from childhood.

Now Grace Churchward loathes the hunt and all its traditions. 'Bob and I were brainwashed by our backgrounds,' she told me. 'When we met we were middle aged. We had both been married before. We were both at the same stage. We were starting to realise that we had spent our lives doing something that was hypocritical – something that was indefensible. And this drew us together and we got strength from each other.'

I asked Mrs Churchward how her late husband had been treated by the hunting community once he had denounced the sport to which they were devoted.

'Oh, when Bob's coat stopped being pink – when it became white like it always should have been – they tried to crucify him. They tried to crucify both of us,' Mrs Churchward told me. 'I have rarely seen a man so persecuted for sticking to his beliefs.'

'What sort of a man was your husband?' I asked her. 'He was a gentle man,' she said. 'And I don't mean he was a gentleman. Of course he was that too . . . But he was the most gentle, kind and courteous human being you could ever meet. I loved him . . . '

'What did he do once he gave up hunting?' I asked. 'He wrote,' she replied. 'He wrote articles and imaginative stories for children. He'd always loved reading even when he was a huntsman. Bob was a scholar by nature. Once he gave up hunting – obviously he had much more time for reading . . . If you are always on a horse chasing a fox you don't have much time for scholarly activities. Once Bob gave up hunting he became one of the best-read men I've ever met. You see Bob was a man who was never born to lead the life that he led . . . Well he was born to lead that life of course . . . That was his trouble. But as a character all that hunting didn't suit him at all.'

'Did he become a much happier human being once he gave up hunting?' I asked her.

'Oh goodness, yes – the man was transformed. He was unsatisfied when he was spending his life destroying animals. He was wretched, he was angry. He was angry with himself. You have to feel angry and unhappy if you know that you are devoting your whole life to doing something which is cruel and repulsive.'

'But do many people who hunt feel that?' I asked.

'They don't feel it consciously. Otherwise they wouldn't go on. But they know it unconsciously. Even when I was hunting, all the time I always really knew it was wrong. I knew it secretly in my heart. But I was irrational. I let my brain defend everything that I did. There were all those wicked excuses. One was doing such good to the farmers . . . One was being so kind to the poor animal . . . One was saving it from a fate worse than death. Oh, you must know all the rubbish that the hunting world tells its children. And it's very easy to indoctrinate children with the most evil attitudes.

Just look round the world and you can see what humans can make their children think is right. You can see what they can make their children do. And I was indoctrinated very early. Bob was too. We were only fortunate that we met when we were starting to question everything that the world we'd been brought up in had taught us.'

'How did the hunting community persecute you when you both changed your views?'

'Our friends, or the friends we had *thought* were friends, ostracised us. A few wonderful real friends remained loyal, of course – and those are the ones I still have. But our telephone certainly stopped ringing. Bob and I didn't mind being ostracised – we had each other. It was the hatred, the malice, that was really interesting. We knew that our new position would never be popular, but we were innocents. We never expected that we would be loathed and reviled to such a degree. The venom, the fury, the spite, the aggression – it took us by surprise.'

Mrs Churchward asked me to remember the upper-class ethics that were prevalent in Great Britain in the 1930s in hunting, shooting and fishing circles. If you didn't like fox-hunting you were seen as vicious and dangerous. You obviously hated the British Empire. You wanted to bring about its downfall.

'After Bob published *A Master of Hounds Speaks*, they saw him as a traitor and they loathed him for that. But I think that they almost hated me more. They seemed to think that I'd influenced him. They painted me as the evil seductress who had brought about the ruin of a fine man. Bob had already turned against fox-hunting before he met me. He was always going that way. But they couldn't face that. Someone had to be blamed for his defection and they liked to blame a woman. They tried to make out that Bob was a poor weak man who had fallen into the clutches of a dominant female.'

When Mrs Churchward referred to the hunting community she called them 'they'. Her 'they' sounded so formidable and powerful. It was a 'they' that had all the relentlessness of a pack.

'It was very curious,' she said to me, 'when Bob was hunting they all admired him for being so strong. And he really was a strong man. He was a very courageous character. I've never known a man so fearless. But once he gave up hunting all his enemies sneered at him and called him weak and cowardly.'

After her late husband took a public position against fox-hunting, Grace Churchward was deluged with hate mail and abusive telephone calls. From her account, it sounded as if she had been treated as the Wallis Windsor of the hunting field. She'd been blamed for bringing about the abdication of one of the great Kings of the sport. Wallis Windsor also received mail-bags full of poison-pen letters. Robert Churchward had chosen to resign his Mastership of the South Shropshire Hounds; the Duke of Windsor chose to leave the British throne. In both cases it was the women who were seen as the ones to blame.

'You couldn't believe the nasty rumours they spread about both of us. They said we had gone mad, were liars and ought to be locked up. Whatever cruel things that human beings can say about other human beings – they said them about us.'

Mrs Churchward told me that the hunting community had made a point of accusing her husband of lying incorrigibly when he disclosed that trapped foxes were often brought to the meets in bags and released with pads slashed by penknives. They had also denounced him as a man prone to fantasy when he had claimed that it was common practice to breed foxes in artificial earths for the sole purpose of creating prey for the huntsman. The hunt had found this last claim by Robert Churchward very threatening. It jeopardised the whole image of the huntsman as devoting himself to serving the interests of the farmer.

In order to counter his accusations they had insisted that if such practices had ever existed they had done so only with the

South Shropshire Hounds in the period when Robert Churchward had been their master. 'So likely,' his widow said. 'So likely that only the South Shropshire Hounds went in for all that horror.'

Soon after the publication of Robert Churchward's incendiary little pamphlet, a stranger wrote a letter in which he challenged her late husband to a duel. 'The silly idiot soon faded away after Bob accepted his challenge. We never heard from that pathetic creature again!'

In the same period the sporting magazine *Horse and Hound* published an article that was so libellous that Robert Churchward felt obliged to sue.

'I can't even remember what they said about Bob in *Horse and Hound*. I just remember that it was horrible and cruel and untrue. It was such a nightmarish time. Someone actually chased me with a riding-crop! I remember people shouting abuse at me. They called me every obscene name under the sun. "Bloody little earth stopper!" they shouted.' I couldn't understand this insult and asked Grace Churchward to explain it. I assumed it had to be sexual, but still failed to get the point.

She told me that it was a very in-group hunting insult. 'An earth-stopper blocks up the fox's "earth" so that he is trapped. I think they thought I'd done the same thing to Bob. I had put him in a position where his escape route was blocked and the poor man couldn't get out to go on fox-hunting!'

'Did your husband win his libel suit against *Horse and Hound*?' I asked her.

'Yes, he did. Bob won. He was warned that the judge who presided over his case was bound to be a pro-hunting man. No one thought he had much hope but he went ahead and he won . . . The judge may well have been a pro-hunting man but he couldn't really make a nonsense of British law just because he disapproved of someone who had given up being a Master of Hounds.'

To the end of Churchward's life the hunt kept insisting that he had recanted.

'Bob was so ill before he died that he couldn't make a statement every time some anti-blood sports issue came up. They took his silence as a sign that he had suffered a death-bed conversion like a frightened lapsed Catholic begging for the priest. But that man never recanted for one second. I nursed him right through his last illness and I know that he adhered to his convictions until he died. He couldn't always speak up on every issue. When Bob was dying he was often literally too ill to speak. He had a stroke . . . Towards the end he was too ill to say anything.'

Grace Churchward longs to see fox-hunting replaced by drag-hunting. She says, 'Nowadays, when we have advanced to the microchip, we should progress from the barbarism of hunting a fox with hounds and turn to the drag hunt.'

In the drag hunt a rider gallops across the countryside and lays an artificial trail for the hounds. He sets a course by dragging a bag that has been saturated in a substance resembling the scent of a fox.

'I don't suppose they will ever settle for the drag hunt,' she said, 'but it could give them just the same fun – just the same excitement. They could still have the wonderful picturesque meet and they wouldn't have to give up the champagne stirrup cup. They could have exactly the same costumes, the same hunting kit – all the same paraphernalia. The drag hunt would be much more exciting for the riders – you wouldn't have all that boring hanging around while you wait for the hounds to find a fox.'

Grace Churchward would like to see the drag hunt replace fox-hunting because the riders would never have 'blank days'. A 'blank day' is one in which the hounds never find a fox at all. There is no chase. The 'field' goes home depressed.

'Blank days are very dangerous from the animals' point of view,' she said. 'If a hunt has too many blank days, they get extremely worried. They become frightened that they will get a bad reputation and lose their subscribers. They get tempted to hunt "bagged" foxes and then you have all that horror.'

The terrier man would have no function in the drag hunt, which she feels would be an enormous blessing.

'Oh I know what they say to that,' she said. 'Drag-hunting can never be the same. But why couldn't it be the same? They could have all the same grooms and all the same horse-boxes. Everything could be the same – except they wouldn't have the cruelty.'

Apart from any moral considerations, Grace Churchward feels that drag-hunting has many practical advantages over the traditional hunt. 'In a drag hunt you don't get so many accidents. You don't get hidden wire in the hedges. You don't get the hounds running over main roads and railway lines.'

She also thinks that the drag hunt would do much less damage to the countryside. 'You wouldn't have the horses galloping over young crops and all that. Oh, I know what they say to that too,' she said. 'What are you going to do about the fox? He has to be controlled. And foxes do attack poultry – we know that.'

She felt that the fox could be controlled very easily if the Ministry of Agriculture used skilled marksmen with guns that had telescopic lenses, and if the hunt were to stop breeding foxes for their own purposes there would be far fewer foxes and they would need much less controlling.

'It's the hypocrisy of hunting that I abhor because it is absolutely unnecessary,' Grace Churchward said. 'I just hope I live to see the day when fox-hunting is abolished and replaced by the drag hunt. Then I'll feel that poor Bob's battle was not fought in vain.'

# 19

# Myths and Legends of the Hunt

*'The only good thing for men therefore is to be diverted from thinking of what they are, either by some occupation which takes their mind off it or by some novel and agreeable passion which keeps them busy, like gambling, hunting.'*

Pascal

Many superstitions and myths have grown up around the fox-hunt and it is interesting that the themes of guilt and retribution are ever present.

The Gormanstown family is meant to be plagued by the curse of the foxes. It is reputed that the current heir to this ancient Irish peerage knows that he is on the brink of death if he sees a couple of foxes dancing for joy outside his house. Viscount Gormanstown is now the head of this fox-accursed family. He has had several nasty shocks when he has looked from his window and seen a couple of foxes dancing blithely on the lawn.

Legend claims that the late Duke of Beaufort spotted three foxes sitting on his father's grave in the cemetery at Badminton just before he took his troubled rest there. Henry Beaufort had two heart attacks before he suffered the third which killed him. Three foxes, three coronaries.

The vast Irish Palladian mansion, Castletown, stands by the River Liffey in County Kildare. A cracked mirror hangs on the wall in the dining-room. The marble in front of the beautiful Georgian fireplace is cracked in half. In the eighteenth century the house was owned by a Lady Louisa Connolly – a passionately keen huntswoman.

One day, so the legend tells us, Lady Louisa was out with the hounds as usual. She noticed to her excitement and interest that an exceptionally handsome stranger had suddenly joined the field. Lady Louisa had never seen a rider who was so fearless. She was overwhelmed as she noted his skills as a rider. She fell in love with his dash and expertise.

Soon Lady Louisa and the mysterious newcomer left the rest of the field behind them. They were up with the hounds together and hunted alone until nightfall. They were the only couple to be 'in at the kill'.

Lady Louisa invited the handsome huntsman to come back to Castletown to dine with her. He accepted her invitation with eagerness. His hostess shivered when he kissed her hand.

At dinner Lady Louisa placed the glamorous stranger on her right-hand side in the place of honour. She was on the point of raising her glass of champagne to him when the footmen came to pull off the hunting boots of her guests, it being the custom at Castletown that boots were removed at table. Lady Louisa had found that the huntsmen were always ravenously hungry when they returned from the pleasures of the chase. They wanted their food, and they wanted their wine. They were not men who would 'brook any delay'.

After Lady Louisa had made her flirtatious toast to the stranger, she happened to look down beneath the dining-room table. She gave a piercing scream and her guests all looked at her with dismay. A footman had just knelt to remove one of the stranger's hunting boots. Lady Louisa saw that coming out of his immaculate white hunting breeches was not a foot – but a cloven hoof!

The Devil just sat there laughing as he watched the consternation and terror of the guests. He was wearing a scarlet coat and he was drinking champagne and it was clear that he felt he was truly 'in the pink'.

Terrified servants were sent panting down the elm-lined drive to Celbridge, the nearest village. When they came back they were accompanied by the local priest. His eyes were bulging with fear and he was clutching a copy of the Holy Bible.

The priest hurled the sacred book at the Devil, but the Devil, being demonic, quickly dodged. The misfired Bible hit a mirror that was hanging on the wall. The mirror split in two. The Devil went on laughing and strolled over to the Georgian fireplace. He lifted up the tails of his scarlet hunting coat and warmed his backside by the fire.

The demented priest retrieved the fallen Bible and once more hurled it at the satanic huntsman. This time the priest was successful. The sacred book hit the Devil and he howled. He stamped his cloven hoof in his rage. He seemed to be in hellish pain. He smashed the marble hearth in front of the fireplace. There was an explosion and a ball of fire and apparently lots of smoke. The Devil vanished up the chimney and was not seen again.

Sceptics have questioned the veracity of this ancient tale. They have suggested that it only originated because everyone who attended that historic Castletown dinner was disgracefully drunk. The cynics insinuate that Lady Louisa was drunk, as were all her guests, and her butler and footmen. They suspect that even the priest was deplorably inebriated, and that in all the bacchic confusion, things seemed to happen which never really did.

But a broken mirror still hangs in the dining-room at Castletown. The marble hearth in front of the Georgian fireplace is still cracked. The dining-room has an eerie and menacing atmosphere. It is certainly not a place where any sensitive person would choose to spend the night.

The theme of the Devil appearing as huntsman runs through many hunting myths and tales of the supernatural. There are countless anonymous horror tales about hunting which vary in their details, but the moral is always the same. The basic plot of these legends goes like this . . .

An individual rider has the best day's hunting that he's ever experienced. The scent is perfect, foxes abound, he enjoys the longest runs, the huntsman directs his hounds with an unparalleled brilliance. At the end of the day the jubilant rider leaves the rest of the field behind. He finds himself riding alone with the superb huntsman and the hounds. All is well until it starts to grow dark and the rider suddenly notices there is something menacing in the way that the hounds are baying. The 'music' that they are making is not the 'music' of the normal hound.

In all these gothic hunting tales, there comes the dreadful moment of recognition. The brilliant huntsman turns, and looks back over his shoulder. His mouth is a crooked twist of evil. He laughs at his follower. The poor rider gives the same scream of horror that was given by Lady Louisa. He realises that he has been seduced into riding alone with the Devil. He starts to tremble once he understands that he is following the Hounds of Hell and they are leading him down to the Inferno.

These morality fables of the fox-hunt in which the pleasures of fox-hunting lead the individual down a primrose path to his own destruction make for entertaining reading. They may well derive from the thunderous denunciations of blood sports by the Puritans.

There is another very contradictory theme that also runs through ancient hunting literature, which has continued to modern times. This recurring motif insists that the joy that the huntsman takes in the chase purifies him and purges him of sin.

Edward, Duke of York, writing *circa* 1400, described the huntsman returning from the chase. 'And when he hath well eaten and drunk he shall be glad and well, and well at his ease. And then shall he take the air in the evening for the great heat that he hath had. And then he shall go and drink and lie in his bed in fair fresh clothes and shall sleep well and steadfastly all the night without any evil thoughts of sins, wherefore I say that hunters go into Paradise when they die, and live in the world more joyfully than other men . . . ' The Duke seemed to see the night clothes of huntsmen as fresher than those of other men.

Another ancient ballad of a later date echoes the same belief that the joy of the huntsman frees him from sin:

*Joys of Hunting*

*For myself I cannot fancy*
*A more happy state of mind*
*Than his who rides well up to hounds*
*While care sits on behind.*

*There is nothing to allure him*
*In the vanities of life*
*Ambition, scandal, politics,*
*Hatred, emulation, strife . . .*

*And all those dire diseases*
*Men really good, discard,*
*Are merged in forgetfulness*
*When hounds are running hard.*

Surtees believed that fox-hunters made better husbands than other men. When he tried to find one single example of a bad fox-hunting husband he was happy to say that he had failed. He thought that a sportsman husband returned from the chase with 'his mind enlarged, his spirits raised, his body refreshed . . . If he has had a good run and been carried to his liking his harvest-moon heart loves all the world.'

Surtees also felt that the hazards of the hunting field were erotically stimulating, and that the huntsman pays more sexual attention to his wife than the non-hunter. 'There is no doubt that the roughings and scramblings, and wettings and rollings and muddings of the morning all tend to make a man enjoy the comforts of home and the pleasure of female company in the evening.'

Siegfried Sassoon has perhaps best described the sense of purifying joy that the huntsman experiences:

> The mornings I remember most zestfully were those which took us up to the chalk downs. To watch the day breaking from purple to dazzling gold while we trotted up a deep-rutted lane; to inhale the early freshness when we were on the sheep-cropped uplands; to stare back at the low country with its cock-crowing farms and mist-coiled waterways; thus to be riding out with a sense of spacious discovery – was it not something stolen from the lie-a-bed world and the luckless city workers – even though it ended in nothing more than the killing of a leash of fox-cubs (for whom, to tell the truth, I felt an unconfessed sympathy)?

His joy in hunting continued to sustain Sassoon when he went off to fight in the First World War, from which he was to return broken, badly wounded and mentally deranged. In France he staged a mock hunt with his young lover, still in earshot of the guns and shells which were blasting away at the trenches:

> But even then it wasn't easy to think of dying . . . Still less so when Dick was with me, and we were having an imitation hunt. I used to pretend to be hunting a pack of hounds, with him as my whipper-in. I would go solemnly through a wood, cheering imaginary hounds. After an imaginary fox had been found, away we'd scuttle, looking in vain for a fence to jump, making imaginary casts after an imaginary check, and losing our fox when the horses had done enough galloping. An imaginary kill didn't appeal to me, somehow.

If one reads the letters of many young British officers who fought in that gruesome war, it's easy to get the impression that fox-hunting was the cause that they felt they were fighting for. Many of these ill-fated young men continued to smuggle back their 'subs' or subscriptions to the hunt that they supported, at a point in the war when they only had to take a look at the carnage all around them to know that it was unlikely they would ever get the chance to hunt again.

I once saw a hunting print dating from 1915. It portrayed a British soldier lying in a trench. Both his legs had been blown off by a shell and he had a blood-soaked bandage round his head. Beside him there was a horrible pile of the dead and mutilated bodies of his fellow fighters.

The soldier was gazing up at the sky with a rapturous expression. High up in the hunting print, in the elevated position in which the Virgin Mary is often placed in a religious picture, there was a scarlet-coated huntsman riding blithely with his hounds through some heavenly and snowy-white clouds. The huntsman was seen as God. He represented goodness, hope and joy in a brutal and painful world.

The intriguing, rather ponderous definition of 'hunting' in the *Encyclopaedia Britannica* also supports the view that the sport has a civilising effect on its practitioners.

> The circumstances which render necessary the habitual pursuit of wild animals, either as a means of subsistence or for self-defence, generally accompany a phase of human progress distinctly inferior to the pastoral and agricultural stages; resorted to as a recreation, on the other hand, the practice of the chase in most cases indicates a considerable degree of civilisation, and sometimes ultimately becomes the almost distinctive employment of the classes which are possessed of most leisure and wealth.

Karen Blixen, the Danish writer who wrote under the

name Isaac Dinesen, would not have found any reason to quarrel with this ultra-British definition of the humanising value of 'the practice of the chase'.

Dinesen exalted the values of big game hunting, as she lived for many years in Africa. But her conviction that hunting was a civilising occupation that brought out the best in mankind was as strong as that of the compilers of the *Encyclopaedia Britannica*, and she expressed it with eloquence. 'The person who can take delight in a sweet tune without wanting to learn it, in a beautiful woman without wanting to possess her, in a magnificent head of game without wanting to shoot it – has not got a human heart.'

The notion that the hunter has more heart than the non-hunter creates a chasm that divides the blood sport lovers from the 'anti's'. Both sides feel that they are fighting for the right to retain humane and decent values, and as they see these values very differently their conflict has no easy resolution. It is because the issue of fox-hunting is a moral one that it continues to stir up controversy in an age when it could seem to have little national relevance.

Throughout history, hunting has been seen as an excellent preparation for war. Xenophon, the pupil of Socrates and hero of the Persian wars, wrote that hunting 'affords the best training for war', and his opinion has been supported down the ages. The Duke of Wellington made all his young officers hunt in the Shires so that they would acquire 'that particular brand of dash, fire and an eye for country'.

The leading military academy in Great Britain, Sandhurst, still has its own pack of hounds. This infuriates many Britons who oppose the sport. They resent the fact that the pack is subsidised by their taxes.

The huntsman is more hated by many people today than he has been in previous generations because he is more feared – he is seen as a figure who spends his life in constant preparation for war. Nuclear weapons have changed the romantic and patriotic image that 'going to war' once had, and the huntsman has lost much of his glamour for those who fear war.

'Fox-hunters and Nuke-lovers – they all have the same mentality,' a worker for the Campaign for Nuclear Disarmament said to me.

James Teacher, who was joint Master of the Quorn, and still makes a tedious, time-consuming drive from Kent to Leicester in order to hunt with his beloved pack twice a week, denies that there is any connection between fox-hunting and the bellicose mentality.

'They think that hunting is to do with cruelty – but it's nothing to do with that. It's to do with beauty.'

He said that he'd been riding back after a day's hunting with the Quorn. The hooves of his horse were striking sparks on the road as he went hacking home in the dusk. He'd asked himself why he loved fox-hunting with such a passion, and he had decided that it was because he loved to hear the sound of hooves and see the beauty of those sparks.

'Hunting satisfies all the senses,' he said. 'All the smells you get out hunting are beautiful. You get the sweat of a tired horse. You get the smell of leather, all the saddles, and so on. You get the smells of the countryside in the early morning, fresh wet earth, cattle – all that. Then all the noises of hunting are beautiful, the sound of the horn, the music of the hounds, the clop of hooves on a road. The neighing, the snorting, it's all wonderful to the ear. Then hunting is so beautiful visually. When you see the hounds going up a frosty hill – they are such superb animals. It may sound corny. But there isn't a more beautiful sight. I think that most people only hunt because they love beauty – not because they love cruelty. There's a modern misconception about hunting.'

The late Poet Laureate, John Masefield, gave the most forceful, and mystical expression to the view that 'the practice of the chase' is a vital force for human good. 'Hunting makes more people happy than anything else I know,' he wrote in *Reynard the Fox*. 'When people are happy together I am quite certain they build up something eternal, something both beautiful and divine which weakens the power of all evil things upon the life of men and women.'

If John Masefield was correct in his assessment, it will be a grim day for Great Britain if the groups that oppose the blood sport ever succeed in bringing about its legal abolition.

The primitive fables of the fox-hunt in which the Devil appears as the beautiful huntsman, and the evil tempter, still have to be considered. They appear to spring from a buried guilt that lies rock-heavy on the human conscience. This conscience finds it insufferable and devilish that the human being can derive quite so much pleasure from causing pain to a defenceless animal.

## A NOTE ON THE AUTHOR

Caroline Blackwood was born in Ulster in 1931. She was educated in Switzerland and later worked for the Hulton Press in London. She moved to New York where she lived for fourteen years and she now lives in London with her three children.

## A NOTE ON THE TYPE

Bembo, the typeface used in this book, is a recutting of a type used by the scholar-printer Aldus Manutius.

In 1495 Aldus set up a press in Venice, which had for some time been an important printing centre, and in the same year published a tract by Pietro Bembo in which the type now known as Bembo first appeared.

Bembo (1470–1547), in spite of having a finger cut off in a quarrel as a youth and being described as having 'fed on amorous and social opportunities', rose to become a Cardinal as well as one of the most eloquent spokesmen of the Venetian literary world of the early sixteenth century.

The type, inspired by the calligraphic style of the handwritten manuscripts of the day, was extremely influential, being the origin of a style of type design known as 'Old Face' – a style that spread throughout Europe in the sixteenth century, and remains one of the most frequently used type styles to this day.

The work of Aldus' press made Venice a leading source for the dissemination of Greek literature throughout the West and thus made a significant contribution to the Renaissance.